Introduction

Neville Goddard's Interpretation of Scripture is a compilation from Neville's 10 books and a few of his lectures. In my opinion Neville decoded the Bible in such a light that the truth can finally be known.

Many who enjoy the old familiar verses of Scripture are discouraged when they themselves try to read the Bible as they would any other book because, quite excusably, they do not understand that the Bible is written in the language of symbolism.

Not knowing that all of its characters are personifications of the laws and functions of mind; that the Bible is psychology rather than history, they puzzle their brains over it for a while and then give up.

It is all too mystifying.

To understand the significance of its imagery, the reader of the Bible must be imaginatively awake. - Neville Goddard

David Allen

Editors note: All scripture is italicized. I purposely left the verses out so the focus can be on interpretation of the bible and not the bible itself. For those who like to know verses they can easily be Googled.

Neville Goddard's

Interpretation of Scripture

Unlocking The Secrets of The Bible

Edited and Complied
By
David Allen

"Ye shall know the truth, and the truth shall make you free."

Copyright © 2018

Copyright © 2018 by Shanon Allen / David Allen

All rights reserved. No part of this publication may be reproduced, distributed, or transmitted in any form or by any means, including photocopying, recording, or other electronic or mechanical methods, without the prior written permission of the publisher, except in the case of brief quotations embodied in critical reviews and certain other noncommercial uses permitted by copyright law.
Printed in the United States of America.

First Printing, May 2018

ISBN: 978-0-9995435-4-2

Visit Us At **NevilleGoddardBooks.com** for a complete listing of all our books and **1000's of Free Books to Read online and download.**

Copyright © 2018

Neville Goddard's Interpretation of Scripture

"So shall My word be that goeth forth out of My mouth; it shall not return unto Me void, but it shall accomplish that which I please, and it shall prosper in the thing whereto I sent it."

Man can decree a thing and it will come to pass.

Man has always decreed that which has appeared in his world. He is today decreeing that which is appearing in his world and he shall continue to do so as long as man is conscious of being man.

Nothing has ever appeared in man's world, but what man decreed that it should. This you may deny; but try as you will, you cannot disprove it for this decreeing is based upon a changeless principle.

Man does not command things to appear by his words, which are, more often than not, a confession of his doubts and fears.

Decreeing is ever done in consciousness.

Every man automatically expresses that which he is conscious of being. Without effort or the use of words, at every moment of time, man is commanding himself to be and to possess that which he is conscious of being and possessing.

This changeless principle of expression is dramatized in all the Bibles of the world.

The writers of our sacred books were illumined mystics, past masters in the art of psychology. In telling the story of the soul, they personified this impersonal principle in the form of a historical document both to preserve it and to hide it from the eyes of the uninitiated.

Today, those to whom this great treasure has been entrusted, namely, the priesthoods of the world, have forgotten that the Bibles are psychological dramas representing the consciousness of man; in their blind forgetfulness, they now teach their followers to worship its characters as men and women who actually lived in time and space.

When man sees the Bible as a great psychological drama, with all of its characters and actors as the personified qualities and attributes of his own consciousness, then and then only will the Bible reveal to him the light of its symbology.

~~~~~~~~

The Bible proves beyond the shadow of a doubt that Moses and the prophets were in one hundred per cent accord as to the identity and nature of God. And Jesus' life and teachings are in agreement with the findings of the prophets of old.

Moses discovered God to be man's awareness of being, when he declared these little understood words,

"I AM hath sent me unto you."

David sang in his psalms,

"Be still and know that I AM God."

Isaiah declared,

"I AM the Lord and there is none else. There is no God beside me. I girded thee, though thou hast not known me. I form the light, and create darkness; I make peace, and create evil. I the Lord do all these things."

The awareness of being as God is stated hundreds of times in the New Testament.

Neville Goddard's Interpretation of Scripture

To name but a few:

> "*I AM the shepherd"*
> *I AM the door"*
> *I AM the resurrection and the life"*
> *I AM the way"*
> *I AM the Alpha and Omega"*
> *I AM the beginning and the end"*
> *"Whom do you say that I AM?"*

It is not stated,

> *"I, Jesus, am the door. I, Jesus am the way,"*

nor is it said,

> *"Whom do you say that I, Jesus, am?"*

It is clearly stated,

> *"I AM the way."*

The awareness of being is the door through which the manifestations of life pass into the world of form.

Consciousness is the resurrecting power, resurrecting that which man is conscious of being. Man is ever out picturing that which he is conscious of being. This is the truth that makes man free, for man is always self-imprisoned or self-freed.

If you, the reader, will give up all of your former beliefs in a God apart from yourself, and claim God as your awareness of being, as Jesus and the prophets did, you will transform your world with the realization that,

> *"I and my father are one."*

This statement,

"I and my father are one, but my father is greater than I,"

seems very confusing, but if interpreted in the light of what we have just said concerning the identity of God, you will find it very revealing.

Consciousness, being God, is as 'Father.' The thing that you are conscious of being is the 'son' bearing witness of his 'father.'

It is like the conceiver and its conceptions. The conceiver is ever greater than his conceptions yet ever remains one with his conception.

~~~~~~~~~

If man would give up his belief in a God apart from himself, recognize his awareness of being to be God (this awareness fashions itself in the likeness and image of its conception of itself), he would transform his world from a barren waste to a fertile field of his own liking.

The day man does this he will know that he and his Father are one, but his Father is greater than he.

He will know that his consciousness of being is one with that which he is conscious of being, but that his unconditioned consciousness of being is greater than his conditioned state or his conception of himself.

When man discovers his consciousness to be the impersonal power of expression, which power eternally personifies itself in his conceptions of himself, he will assume and appropriate that state of consciousness which he desires to express; in so doing he will become that state in expression.

"Ye shall decree a thing and it shall come to pass"

can now be told in this manner:

You shall become conscious of being or possessing a thing and you shall express or possess that which you are conscious of being.

The law of consciousness is the only law of expression.

~~~~~~~~~

"If any man should ever come, saying, 'Look here or look there,'
believe them not, for the kingdom of God is within you."

Heaven is within you. Therefore, when it is recorded that

"He went unto his father,"

it is telling you that he rose in consciousness to the point where he was just conscious of being, thus transcending the limitations of his present conception of himself, called 'Jesus.'

In the awareness of being all things are possible, he said,

"You shall decree a thing and it shall come to pass."

This is his decreeing, rising in consciousness to the naturalness of being the thing desired. As he expressed it,

"And I, if I be lifted up, I shall draw all men unto me."

If I be lifted up in consciousness to the naturalness of the thing desired I will draw the manifestation of that desire unto me. For he states,

"No man comes unto me save the father within me draws him, and I and my father are one."

Therefore, consciousness is the father that is drawing the manifestations of life unto you.

~~~~~~~~~

Prayer, like sleep, is also an entrance into the subconscious.

"When you pray, enter into your closet, and when you have shut your door, pray to your Father which is in secret and your
Father which is in secret shall reward you openly."

Prayer is an illusion of sleep which diminishes the impression of the outer world and renders the mind more receptive to suggestion from within. The mind in prayer is in a state of relaxation and receptivity akin to the feeling attained just before dropping off to sleep.

Prayer is not so much what you ask for, as how you prepare for its reception.

> *"Whatsoever things ye desire, when ye pray believe that you have received them, and ye shall have them."*

The only condition required is that you believe that your prayers are already realized.

Your prayer must be answered if you assume the feeling that would be yours were you already in possession of your objective. The moment you accept the wish as an accomplished fact, the subconscious finds means for its realization.

To pray successfully then, you must yield to the wish, that is, feel the wish fulfilled.

The perfectly disciplined man is always in tune with the wish as an accomplished fact. He knows that consciousness is the one and only reality, that ideas and feelings are facts of consciousness and are as real as objects in space; therefore he never entertains a feeling which does not contribute to his happiness, for feelings are the causes of the actions and circumstances of his life.

~~~~~~~~~

"I AM the way".

"I AM the resurrection".

Consciousness is the way as well as the power which resurrects and expresses all that man will ever be conscious of being.

Turn from the blindness of the uninitiated man who attempts to express and possess those qualities and things which he is not conscious of being and possessing; and be as the illumined mystic who decrees, on the basis of this changeless law.

Consciously claim yourself to be that which you seek; appropriate the consciousness of that which you see; and you too will know the status of the true mystic, as follows:

I became conscious of being it. I am still conscious of being it. And I shall continue to be conscious of being it until that which I am conscious of being is perfectly expressed.

> "Yes, I shall decree a thing and it shall come to pass."

~~~~~~~~~

"You must be born again."

If you are dissatisfied with your present expression in life the only way to change it, is to take your attention away from that which seems so real to you and rise in consciousness to that which you desire to be.

You cannot serve two masters, therefore to take your attention from one state of consciousness and place it upon another is to die to one and live to the other.

~~~~~~~~~

The question,

"Whom do you say that I AM?"

is not addressed to a man called 'Peter' by one called 'Jesus.' This is the eternal question addressed to one's self by one's true being. In other words,

"Whom do you say that you are?"

For your conviction of yourself, your opinion of yourself, will determine your expression in life. He states,

"You believe in God, believe also in me."

In other words, it is the me within you that is this God.

~~~~~~~~~

**"Ye shall know the truth,
and the truth shall make you free."**

The truth that sets man free is the knowledge that his consciousness is the resurrection and the life, that his consciousness both resurrects and makes alive all that he is conscious of being.

> Apart from consciousness, there is neither resurrection nor life.

When man gives up his belief in a God apart from himself and begins to recognize his awareness of being to be God, as did Jesus and the prophets, he will transform his world with the realization,

> *"I and My Father are one"*

> but

> *"My Father is greater than I."*

He will know that his consciousness is God and that which he is conscious of being is the Son bearing witness of God, the Father.

The conceiver and the conception are one, but the conceiver is greater than his conception.

~~~~~~~~~

Praying is seen to be recognizing yourself to be that which you now desire, rather than its accepting form of petitioning a God that does not exist for that which you now desire.

So can't you see why the millions of prayers are unanswered?

> Men pray to a God that does not exist.

For instance: To be conscious of being poor and to pray to a God for riches is to be rewarded with that which you are conscious of being, which is poverty.

Prayers to be successful must be claiming rather than begging, so if you would pray for riches turn from your picture of poverty by denying the very evidence of your senses and assume the nature of being wealthy.

We are told,

"When you pray go within in secret and shut the door. And that which your father sees in secret, with that will he reward you openly."

We have identified the 'father' to be the awareness of being. We have also identified the 'door' to be the awareness of being.

So 'shutting the door' is shutting out that which 'I' AM now aware of being and claiming myself to be that which 'I' desire to be. The very moment my claim is established to the point of conviction, that moment I begin to draw unto myself the evidence of my claim.

Do not question the how of these things appearing, for no man knows that way. That is, no manifestation knows how the things desired will appear.

Consciousness is the way or door through which things appear.

He said,

"I AM the way"

not 'I,' John Smith, am the way, but "I AM", the awareness of being, is the way through which the thing shall come.

~~~~~~~~~

The signs always follow. They never precede. Things have no reality other than in consciousness. Therefore, get the consciousness first and the thing is compelled to appear.

You are told,

"Seek ye first the kingdom of Heaven and all things shall be added unto you."

Get first the consciousness of the things that you are seeking and leave the things alone.

This is what is meant by

"Ye shall decree a thing and it shall come to pass."

Apply this principle and you will know what it is to

"prove me and see."

~~~~~~~~~

"Before Abraham was, I AM."

Yes, I was aware of being before I became aware of being man, and in that day when I shall cease to be conscious of being man I shall still be conscious of being.

The consciousness of being is not dependent upon being anything. It preceded all conceptions of itself and shall be when all conceptions of itself shall cease to be.

"I AM the beginning and the end".

That is, all things or conceptions of myself begin and end in me, but I, the formless awareness, remain forever.

Jesus discovered this glorious truth and declared Himself to be one with God, not the God that man had fashioned, for He never recognized such a God.

Jesus found God to be His awareness of being and so told man that the Kingdom of God and Heaven were within.

When it is recorded that Jesus left the world and went to His Father it is simply stating that He turned His attention from the world of the senses and rose in consciousness to that level which He desired to express.

There He remained until He became one with the consciousness to which He ascended. When He returned to the world of man, He could act with the positive assurance of that which He was conscious of being, a state of consciousness no one but Himself felt or knew that He possessed.

Man who is ignorant of this everlasting law of expression looks upon such happenings as miracles.

To rise in consciousness to the level of the thing desired and to remain there until such level becomes your nature is the way of all seeming miracles.

~~~~~~~~~

The story of Mary is the story of every man. Mary was not a woman, giving birth in some miraculous way to one called 'Jesus.'

Mary is the awareness of being that ever remains virgin, no matter how many desires it gives birth to. Right now look upon yourself as this Virgin Mary, being impregnated by yourself through the medium of desire, becoming one with your desire, to the point of embodying or giving birth to your desire.

For instance: It is said of Mary (whom you now know to be yourself) that she know not a man. Yet she conceived.

That is, you, John Smith, have no reason to believe that that which you now desire is possible, but having discovered your awareness of being to be God, you make this awareness your husband and conceive a man child (manifestation) of the Lord,

> *"For thy maker is thine husband; the Lord of hosts is his name; the Lord God of the whole earth shall he be called."*

Your ideal or ambition, is this conception and the first command to her, which is now to yourself, is

> *"Go, tell no man."*

That is, do not discuss your ambitions or desires with another for the other will only echo your present fears.

> Secrecy is the first law to be observed in realizing your desire.

The second, as we are told in the story of Mary, is to

> *"Magnify the Lord."*

We have identified the Lord as your awareness of being. Therefore, to 'Magnify the Lord' is to revalue or expand one's present conception of one's self to the point where this revaluation becomes natural. When this naturalness is attained you give birth by becoming that which you are one with in consciousness.

The story of creation is given us in digest form in the first chapter of John.

> *"In the beginning was the word."*

Now, this very second, is the 'beginning' spoken of. It is the beginning of an urge, a desire. 'The word' is the desire swimming around in your consciousness, seeking embodiment. The urge of itself has no reality, For, "I AM" or the awareness of being is the only reality. Things live only as long as I AM aware of being them; so to realize one's desire, the second line of this first verse of John must be applied. That is,

> *"And the word was with God."*

The word, or desire, must be fixed or united with consciousness to give it reality. The awareness becomes aware of being the thing desired, thereby nailing itself upon the form or conception and giving life unto its conception, or resurrecting that which was heretofore a dead or unfulfilled desire.

> *"Two shall agree as touching anything and it shall be established on earth."*

This agreement is never made between two persons. It is between the awareness and the thing desired. You are now conscious of being, so you are actually saying to yourself, without using words, "I AM."

Now, if it is a state of health that you are desirous of attaining, before you have any evidence of health in your world, you begin to feel yourself to be healthy. And the very second the feeling "I AM healthy" is attained the two have agreed.

That is, I AM and health have agreed to be one and this agreement ever results in the birth of a child which is the thing agreed upon, in this case, health. And because I made the agreement I express the thing agreed. So you can see why Moses stated,

> *"I AM hath sent me."*

For what being, other than I AM could send you into expression?

None, for

> *"I AM the way, beside me there is no other."*

~~~~~~~~~

Moses stated,

"I AM that I AM."

Now here is something to always bear in mind.

> *"You cannot put new wine in old bottles or new patches upon old garments."*

That is; you cannot take with you into the new consciousness any part of the old man. All of your present beliefs, fears and limitations are weights that bind you to your present level of consciousness. If you would transcend this level you must leave behind all that is now your present self, or conception of yourself.

To do this you take your attention away from all that is now your problem or limitation and dwell upon just being. That is; you say silently but feeling to yourself, *"I AM."*

Do not condition this 'awareness' as yet. Just declare yourself to be, and continue to do so, until you are lost in the feeling of just being, faceless and formless.

When this expansion of consciousness is attained, then, within this formless deep of yourself, give form to the new conception by feeling yourself to be that which you desire to be.

You will find within this deep of yourself all things to be divinely possible. Everything in the world which you can conceive of being, is to you, within this present formless awareness, a most natural attainment.

The invitation given us in the Scriptures is

"to be absent from the body and be present with the Lord."

The 'body' being your former conception of yourself and 'the Lord', your awareness of being. This is what is meant when Jesus said to Nicodemus,

"Ye must be born again for except ye be born again ye cannot enter the kingdom of Heaven."

That is; except you leave behind you your present conception of yourself and assume the nature of the new birth, you will continue to out picture your present limitations.

The only way to change your expressions of life is to change your consciousness. For consciousness is the reality that eternally solidifies itself in the things round about you.

Man's world in its every detail is his consciousness out pictured. You can no more change your environment, or world, by destroying things than you can your reflection by destroying the mirror.

Your environment, and all within it, reflects that which you are in consciousness. As long as you continue to be that in consciousness so long will you continue to out picture it in your world.

"The husband is head of the wife,"

may not be true of man and woman in their earthly relationship but it is true of the conscious and the subconscious, or the male and female aspects of consciousness.

The mystery to which Paul referred when he wrote,

"This is a great mystery...
He that loveth his wife loveth himself... .
And they two shall be one flesh,"

is simply the mystery of consciousness.

Consciousness is really one and undivided but for creation's sake it appears to be divided into two.

The conscious (objective) or male aspect truly is the head and dominates the subconscious (subjective) or female aspect. However, this leadership is not that of the tyrant, but of the lover. So, by assuming the feeling that would be yours were you already in possession of your objective, the subconscious is moved to build the exact likeness of your assumption.

Your desires are not subconsciously accepted until you assume the feeling of their reality, for only through feeling is an idea subconsciously accepted and only through this subconscious acceptance is it ever expressed.

It is easier to ascribe your feeling to events in the world than to admit that the conditions of the world reflect your feeling. However, it is eternally true that the outside mirrors the inside.

"As within so without."

> "A man can receive nothing unless
> it is given him from heaven,"

and

> "The kingdom of heaven is within you."

Nothing comes from without; all things come from within . . from the subconscious.

~~~~~~~~

In the Book of Numbers you will read,

> "In that day there were giants in the land; and we were in our own sight as grasshoppers. And we were in their sight as grasshoppers."

This does not mean a time in the dim past when man had the stature of giants. Today is the day, the eternal now when conditions round about you have attained the appearance of giants (such as unemployed, the armies of your enemy, your problems and all things that seem to threaten you) those are the giant that make you feel yourself to be a grasshopper.

But, you are told,

> "you were first, in your own sight a grasshopper and because of this you were to the giants, a grasshopper."

In other words, you can only be to others what you are first to yourself. Therefore, to revalue yourself and begin to feel yourself to be the giant, a center of power, is to dwarf these former giants and make of them grasshoppers.

~~~~~~~~

"And I, if I be lifted up, I shall draw all men unto Me"

If I be lifted up in consciousness to the naturalness of the thing desired, I shall draw the manifestation of that desire to me.

"No man comes unto Me save the Father within Me draws him",

and

"I and My Father are one."

My consciousness is the Father who draws the manifestation of life to me.

The nature of the manifestation is determined by the state of consciousness in which I dwell. I am always drawing into my world that which I am conscious of being.

If you are dissatisfied with your present expression of life, then you must be born again.

Rebirth is the dropping of that level with which you are dissatisfied and rising to that level of consciousness which you desire to express and possess.

You cannot serve two masters or opposing states of consciousness at the same time. Taking your attention from one state and placing it upon the other, you die to the one from which you have taken it and you live and express the one with which you are united.

Man cannot see how it would be possible to express that which he desires to be by so simple a law as acquiring the consciousness of the thing desired.

The reason for this lack of faith on the part of man is that he looks at the desired state through the consciousness of his present limitations. Therefore, he naturally sees it as impossible of accomplishment.

~~~~~~~~

"I AM the good shepherd and know my sheep and am known of mine. My sheep hear my voice and I know them and they will follow me."

Awareness is the good shepherd. What I am aware of being, is the 'sheep' that follow me. So good a 'shepherd' is your awareness that it has never lost one of the 'sheep' that you are aware of being.

I AM a voice calling in the wilderness of human confusion for such as I AM aware of being, and never shall there come a time when that which I am convinced that I AM shall fail to find me.

"I AM" is an open door for all that I AM to enter. Your awareness of being is lord and shepherd of your life.

So,

"The Lord is my shepherd; I shall not want"

is seen in its true light now to be your consciousness. You could never be in want of proof or lack the evidence of that which you are aware of being.

This being true, why not become aware of being great; God-loving; wealthy; healthy; and all attributes that you admire?

It is just as easy to possess the consciousness of these qualities as it is to possess their opposites for you have not your present consciousness because of your world. On the contrary, your world is what it is because of your present consciousness.

Simple, is it not? Too simple in fact for the wisdom of man that tries to complicate everything.

~~~~~~~~

"Let this mind be in you which was also in Christ Jesus, who being in the form of God, thought it not robbery to be equal with God."

You are that which you believe yourself to be.

Instead of believing in God or in Jesus . . believe you are God or you are Jesus.

"He that believeth on me the works that I do shall he do also"

should be

"He that believes as I believe the works that I do shall he do also."

Jesus found it not strange to do the works of God because he believed himself to be God.

"I and my Father are one."

It is natural to do the works of the one you believe yourself to be. So live in the feeling of being the one you want to be and that you shall be.

When a man believes in the value of the advice given him and applies it, he establishes within himself the reality of success.

~~~~~~~~

"I and my father are one but my father is greater than I."

You are one with your present conception of yourself. But you are greater than that which you are at present aware of being.

Before man can attempt to transform his world he must first lay the foundation,

"I AM the Lord."

That is, man's awareness, his consciousness of being is God. Until this is firmly established so that no suggestion or argument put forward by others can shake it, he will find himself returning to the slavery of his former beliefs.

"If ye believe not that I AM he, ye shall die in your sins."

That is, you shall continue to be confused and thwarted until you find the cause of your confusion.

When you have lifted up the son of man then shall you know that

"I AM he",

that is, that I, John Smith, do nothing of myself, but my father, or that state of consciousness which I am now one with, does the works.

When this is realized every urge and desire that springs within you shall find expression in your world.

"Behold I stand at the door and knock. If any man hear my voice and open the door I will come in to him and sup with him and he with me."

The "I" knocking at the door is the urge.

The door is your consciousness. To open the door is to become one with that that which is knocking by feeling oneself to be the thing desired.

To feel one's desire as impossible is to shut the door or deny this urge expression. To rise in consciousness to the naturalness of the thing felt is to swing wide the door and invite this one into embodiment.

That is why it is constantly recorded that Jesus left the world of manifestation and ascended unto his father.

Jesus, as you and I, found all things impossible to Jesus, as man. But having discovered his father to be the state of consciousness of the thing desired, he but left behind him the "Jesus consciousness" and rose in consciousness to that state desired and stood upon it until he became one with it.

As he made himself one with that, he became that in expression.

~~~~~~~~~

One of the first things man must realize is that it is impossible, in dealing with this spiritual law of consciousness,

"to put new wine into old bottles or new patches on old garments."

That is, you cannot take any part of the present consciousness into the new state. For the state sought is complete in itself and needs no patching. Every level of consciousness automatically expresses itself.

To rise to the level of any state is to automatically become that state in expression. But, in order to rise to the level that you are not now expressing, you must completely drop the consciousness with which you are now identified.

Until your present consciousness is dropped, you will not be able to rise to another level.

Do not be dismayed. This letting go of your present identity is not as difficult as it might appear to be.

~~~~~~~~~

"Thank you, father."

When you come into the joy of thanksgiving so that you actually feel grateful for having received that which is not yet apparent to the senses, you have definitely become one in consciousness with the thing for which you gave thanks.

God (your awareness) is not mocked.

You are ever receiving that which you are aware of being and no man gives thanks for something which he has not received.

"Thank you father"

is not, as it is used by many today a sort of magical formula.

You need never utter aloud the words,

"Thank you, father."

In applying this principle as you rise in consciousness to the point where you are really grateful and happy for having received the thing desired, you automatically rejoice and give thanks inwardly. You have already accepted the gift which was but a desire before you rose in consciousness, and your faith is now the substance that shall clothe your desire.

This rising in consciousness is the spiritual marriage where two shall agree upon being one and their likeness or image is established on earth.

~~~~~~~~~

"Know ye not that ye are the temple of God, and that the Spirit of God dwelleth in you?"

The Spirit of God in you is your imagination, but it sleeps and needs to be awakened, in order to lift you off the bar of the senses where you have so long lain stranded.

The boundless possibilities open to you as you become

"wise as serpents"

is beyond measure. You will select the ideal conditions you want to experience and the ideal environment you want to live in. Experiencing these states in imagination until they have sensory vividness, you will externalize them as surely as the serpent now externalizes its skin.

After you have outgrown them, then, you will cast them off as easily as

"the snake throws her enamell'd skin".

The more abundant life, the whole purpose of Creation, cannot be saved through death and resurrection.

God desired form, so He became man: and it is not enough for us to recognize His spirit at work in creation, we must see His work in form and say that it is good, even though we outgrow the form, forever and ever.

Neville Goddard's Interpretation of Scripture

*"He leads
Through widening chambers of
delight to where
Throbs rapture near an end that
aye recedes, Because His touch is
Infinite and lends
A yonder to all ends."*

*"And, I, if I be lifted up from the earth,
will draw all men unto me."*

If I be lifted up from the evidence of the senses to the state of consciousness I desire to realize and remain in that state until it feels natural, I will form that state around me and all men will see it.

But how to persuade man this is true . . that imaginative life is the only living; that assuming the feeling of the wish fulfilled is the way to the more abundant life and not the compensation of the escapist, that is the problem.

To see as

"though widening chambers of delight"

what living in the realms of imagination means, to appreciate and enjoy the world, one must live imaginatively; one must dream and occupy his dream, then grow and outgrow the dream, forever and ever.

The unimaginative man, who will not lose his life on one level that he may find it on a higher level, is nothing but a Lot's wife, a pillar of self-satisfied salt.

On the other hand, those who refuse form as being unspiritual and who reject incarnation as separate from God are ignorant of the great mystery:

"Great is the mystery, God was manifest in the flesh."

Your life expresses one thing, and one thing only, your state of consciousness.

Everything is dependent upon that. As you, through the medium of imagination, assume a state of consciousness, that state begins to clothe itself in form, It solidifies around you as the serpent's skin ossifies around it. But you must be faithful to the state. You must not go from state to state, but, rather, wait patiently in the one invisible state until it takes on form and becomes an objective fact.

Patience is necessary, but patience will be easy after your first success in shedding the old and growing the new, for we are able to wait according as we have been rewarded by understanding in the past.

Understanding is the secret of patience.

~~~~~~~~~

And God said,

"Let there be a firmament in the midst of the waters."

Yes, let there be a firmness or conviction in the midst of this expanded consciousness by knowing and feeling I AM that, the thing desired.

As you claim and feel yourself to be the thing desired, you are crystallizing this formless liquid light, that you are, into the image and likeness of that which you are conscious of being.

Now that the law of your being has been revealed to you, begin this day to change your world by revaluing yourself. Too long has man held to the belief that he is born of sorrow and must work out his salvation by the sweat of his brow.

Neville Goddard's Interpretation of Scripture

God is impersonal and no respecter of persons.

So long as man continues to walk in this belief of sorrow, so long will he walk in a world of sorrow and confusion, for the world in its every detail, is man's consciousness crystallized.

~~~~~~~~~

"For whatsoever ye ask in my name the same give I unto you."

'Whatsoever' is quite a large measure. It is the unconditional. It does not state if society deems it right or wrong that you should ask it, it rests with you. Do you really want it? Do you desire it? That is all that is necessary.

Life will give it to you is you ask

"in his name."

His name is not a name that you pronounce with the lips. You can ask forever in the name of God or Jehovah or Christ Jesus and you will ask in vain.

'Name' means nature; so, when you ask in the nature of a thing, results ever follow.

To ask in the name is to rise in consciousness and become one in nature with the thing desired, rise in consciousness to the nature of the thing, and you will become that thing in expression.

~~~~~~~~~

"what things soever ye desire, when ye pray, believe that ye receive them and ye shall receive them."

Praying, as we have shown you before, is recognition, the injunction to believe that ye receive is first person, present tense. This means that you must be in the nature of the things asked for before you can receive them.

To get into the nature easily, general amnesty is necessary.

We are told,

> *"Forgive if ye have aught against any,*
> *that your father also, which is in Heaven,*
> *may forgive you. But if ye forgive not,*
> *neither will your father forgive you."*

This may seem to be some personal God who is pleased or displeased with your actions but this is not the case.

Consciousness, being God, if you hold in consciousness anything against man, you are binding that condition in your world.

But to release man from all condemnation is to free yourself so that you may rise to any level necessary; there is therefore, no condemnation to those in Christ Jesus.

Therefore, a very good practice before you enter into your meditation is first to free every man in the world from blame.

For law is never violated and you can rest confidently in the knowledge that every man's conception of himself is going to be his reward.

So you do not have to bother yourself about seeing whether or not man gets what you consider he should get. For life makes no mistakes and always gives man that which man first gives himself.

"There is nothing covered that shall not be uncovered.

That which is spoken in secret shall be proclaimed from the housetops.

That is, your secret convictions of yourself, these secret claims that no man knows of, when really believed, will be shouted from the housetops in your world.

For your convictions of yourself are the words of the God within you, which words are spirit and cannot return unto you void but must accomplish whereunto they are sent.

You are at this moment calling out of the infinite that which you are now conscious of being. And not one word or conviction will fail to find you.

~~~~~~~~~

"I AM" the vine and ye are the branches."

Consciousness is the 'vine,' and those qualities which you are now conscious of being are as 'branches' that you feed and keep alive.

Just as a branch has no life except it be rooted in the vine, so likewise things have no life except you be conscious of them. Just as a branch withers and dies if the sap of the vine ceases to flow towards it, so do things in your world pass away if you take your attention from them, because your attention is as the sap of life that keeps alive and sustains the things of your world.

To dissolve a problem that now seems so real to you all that you do is remove your attention from it. In spite of its seeming reality, turn from it in consciousness. Become indifferent and begin to feel yourself to be that which would be the solution of the problem.

For instance; if you were imprisoned no man would have to tell you that you should desire freedom. Freedom, or rather the desire of freedom would be automatic. So why look behind the four walls of your prison bars?

Take your attention from being imprisoned and begin to feel yourself to be free. Feel it to the point where it is natural and the very second you do so, those prison bars will dissolve. Apply this same principle to any problem.

~~~~~~~~~

All things, when they are admitted, are made manifest by the light: for everything that is made manifest is light.

The "Light" is consciousness. Consciousness is one, manifesting in legions of forms or levels of consciousness.

There is no one that is not all that is, for consciousness, though expressed in an infinite series of levels, is not divisional. There is no real separation or gap in consciousness.

I AM cannot be divided. I may conceive myself to be a rich man, a poor man, a beggar man or a thief, but the center of my being remains the same, regardless of the concept I hold of myself.

At the center of manifestation, there is only one I AM manifesting in legions of forms or concepts of itself and

"I AM that I AM".

I AM is the self-definition of the absolute, the foundation on which everything rests. I AM is the first cause-substance.

I AM is the self-definition of God.

Neville Goddard's Interpretation of Scripture

"I AM hath sent me unto you."

"I AM that I AM."

'Be still and know that I AM God."

I AM is a feeling of permanent awareness. The very center of consciousness is the feeling of I AM. I may forget who I am, where I am, what I am, but I cannot forget that I AM. The awareness of being remains, regardless of the degree of forgetfulness of who, where and what I am.

~~~~~~~~~

"Be ye doers of the word and not hearers only, deceiving your own selves. For if any be a hearer of the word, and not a doer, he is like unto a man beholding his natural face in a glass and goeth his way, and straightway forgetteth what manner of man he was. But whoso looketh into the perfect law of liberty, and continue therein, he being not a forgetful hearer but a doer of the work, this man shall be blessed in his deed."

The word, in this quotation, means idea, concept, or desire.

You deceive yourself by "hearing only" when you expect your desire to be fulfilled through mere wishful thinking.

Your desire is what you want to be, and looking at yourself "in a glass" is seeing yourself in imagination as that person.

Forgetting "what manner of man" you are is failing to persist in your assumption.

The "perfect law of liberty" is the law which makes possible liberation from limitation, that is, the law of assumption. To continue in the perfect law of liberty is to persist in the assumption that your desire is already fulfilled.

You are not a "forgetful hearer" when you keep the feeling of your wish fulfilled constantly alive in your consciousness.

This makes you a "doer of the work", and you are blessed in your deed by the inevitable realization of your desire.

You must be doers of the law of assumption, for without application, the most profound understanding will not produce any desired result. Frequent reiteration and repetition of important basic truths runs through these pages.

Where the law of assumption is concerned . . the law that sets man free . . this is a good thing. It should be made clear again and again even at the risk of repetition. The real truth-seeker will welcome this aid in concentrating his attention upon the law which sets him free.

The parable of the Master's condemnation of the servant who neglected to use the talent given him is clear and unmistakable.

Having discovered within yourself the key to the Treasure House, you should be like the good servant who, by wise use, multiplied by many times the talents entrusted to him.

The talent entrusted to you is the power to consciously determine your assumption. The talent not used, like the limb not exercised, withers and finally atrophies.

What you must strive after is being. In order to do, it is necessary to be. The end of yearning is to be. Your concept of yourself can only be driven out of consciousness by another concept of yourself.

By creating an ideal in your mind, you can identify yourself with it until you become one and the same with the ideal, thereby transforming yourself into it.

The dynamic prevails over the static; the active over the passive. One who is a doer is magnetic and therefore infinitely more creative than any who merely hear.

Be among the doers.

~~~~~~~~

In the Book of Numbers it is recorded,

"There were giants in the land and we were in our own sight as grasshoppers, and we were in their sight as grasshoppers."

Today is the day, the eternal now, when conditions in the world have attained the appearance of giants. The unemployed, the armies of the enemy, business competition etc. are the giants which make you feel yourself to be a helpless grasshopper.

We are told we were first in our own sight helpless grasshoppers and because of this conception of ourselves were to the enemy helpless grasshoppers.

We can be to others only that which we are to ourselves.

Therefore, as we revalue ourselves and begin to feel ourselves to be the giant, a center of power, we automatically change our relationship to the giants, reducing these former monsters to their true place, making them appear to be the helpless grasshoppers.

~~~~~~~~

> *"**Verily I say unto you, inasmuch as ye have done it unto one of the least of these my breathren, Ye have done it unto me.**"*

Every time you exercise your imagination on behalf of another, be it good, bad or indifferent, you have literally done that to Christ, for Christ is awakened Human Imagination.

Through the wise and loving use of imagination, man clothes and feeds Christ, and through ignorant and fearful misuse of imagination, man disrobes and scourges Christ.

> *"let none of you imagine evil in your hearts against your neighbor"...,*

is sound but negative advice.

A man may stop misusing his imagination on the advice of a friend; he may be negatively served by the experience of others and learn not to imagine, but that is not enough. Such lack of use of the creative power of imagination could never clothe and feed Christ.

The purple robe of the Son of God is woven, not by not imagining evil, but by imaging the good; by the active, voluntary and loving use of imagination.

> *"Whatsoever things are of good report; if there be any virtue, and if there be any praise, think on these things."*
> *"King Solomon made himself a chariot of the wood of Lebanon. He made the pillars thereof of silver, the bottom thereof of gold, the covering of it of purple, the midst thereof being paved with love..."*

The first thing we notice is "King Solomon made himself". That is what every man must eventually do . . make himself a chariot of the wood of Lebanon.

By chariot, the writer of this allegory means Mind, in which stands the spirit of Wisdom . . Solomon . . controlling the four functions of Mind that he may build a world of Love and Truth.

*"And Joseph made ready his chariot
and went up to meet Israel his father."*

*"What tributaries follow him to Rome
to grace in captive bonds his chariot wheels?"*

If man does not make himself a chariot of the wood of Lebanon, then his will be like Queen Mab's:

*"She is the fairies' midwife; ...
her chariot is an empty hazelnut."*

The wood of Lebanon was the mystic's symbol of incorruptibility.

To a mystic, It is obvious what King Solomon made himself.

Silver typified knowledge, gold symbolized wisdom, and purple . . clothed or covered the incorruptible Mind, with the red of Love and the blue of Truth.

"And they clothed him with purple."

Incarnate, incorruptible four-fold wisdom, clothed in purple . . Love and Truth . . the purpose of man's experience on earth.

Love is the sage's stone;
It takes gold from the clod;
It turns naught into aught,

> Transforms me into God."
> ... Angelus Silesius

~~~~~~~~~

There are two distinct centers of thought or outlooks on the world possessed by every man.

The Bible speaks of these two outlooks as natural and spiritual.

> *"The natural man receiveth not the things of the Spirit of God: for they are foolishness unto him: neither can he know them, because they are spiritually discerned."*

Man's inner body is as real in the world of subjective experience as his outer physical body is real in the world of external realities, but the inner body expresses a more fundamental part of reality. This existing inner body of man must be consciously exercised and directed. The inner world of thought and feeling to which the inner body is attuned has its real structure and exists in its own higher space.

There are two kinds of movement, one that is according to the inner body and another that is according to the outer body. The movement which is according to the inner body is causal, but the outer movement is under compulsion.

The inner movement determines the outer which is joined to it, bringing into the outer a movement that is similar to the actions of the inner body. Inner movement is the force by which all events are brought to pass. Outer movement is subject to the compulsion applied to it by the movement of the inner body.

Whenever the actions of the inner body match the actions which the outer must take to appease desire, that desire will be realized.

Construct mentally a drama which implies that your desire is realized and make it one which involves movement of self. Immobilize your outer physical self. Act precisely as though you were going to take a nap, and start the predetermined action in imagination.

A vivid representation of the action is the beginning of that action. Then, as you are falling asleep, consciously imagine yourself into the scene. The length of the sleep is not important, a short nap is sufficient, but carrying the action into sleep thickens fancy into fact.

At first your thoughts may be like rambling sheep that have no shepherd. Don't despair. Should your attention stray seventy times seven, bring it back seventy times seven to its predetermined course until from sheer exhaustion it follows the appointed path.

The inner journey must never be without direction. When you take to the inner road, it is to do what you did mentally before you started. You go for the prize you have already seen and accepted.

~~~~~~~~~

Your answer to,

"Whom do you say that I AM"?

ever determines your expression. As long as you are conscious of being imprisoned or diseased, or poor, so long will you continue to out picture or express these conditions.

When man realized that he is now that which he is seeking and begins to claim that he is, he will have the proof of his claim.

This cue is given you in words,

"Whom seek ye?"

And they answered,

"Jesus."

And the voice said,

"I AM he."

'Jesus' here means salvation or savior. You are seeking to be salvaged from that which is not your problem.

"I AM" is he that will save you. If you are hungry, your savior is food. If you are poor, your savior is riches. If you are imprisoned, your savior is freedom. If you are diseased, it will not be a man called Jesus who will save you, but health will become your savior.

Therefore, claim

"I AM he,"

in other words, claim yourself to be the thing desired. Claim it in consciousness, not in words, and consciousness will reward you with your claim.

~~~~~~~~~

You are told,

"You shall find me when you Feel after me."

Well, feel after that quality in consciousness until you feel yourself to be it. When you lose yourself in the feeling of being it, the quality will embody itself in your world.

You are healed from your problem when you touch the solution of it.

"Who has touched me?

For I perceive virtue is gone out of me." Yes, the day you touch this being within you, feeling yourself to be cured or healed, virtues will come out of your very self and solidify themselves in your world as healings.

~~~~~~~~~

"I AM the Lord."

Man must know that his awareness of being is God. Until this is firmly established so that no suggestion or argument of others can shake him, he will find himself returning to the slavery of his former belief.

"If ye believe not that I AM He, ye shall die in your sins."

Unless man discovers that his consciousness is the cause of every expression of his life, he will continue seeking the cause of his confusion in the world of effects, and so shall die in his fruitless search.

"I AM the vine and ye are the branches."

Consciousness is the vine and that which you are conscious of being is as branches that you feed and keep alive.

Just as a branch has no life except it be rooted in the vine, likewise things have no life except you be conscious of them.

Just as a branch withers and dies if the sap of the vine ceases to flow towards it, so do things and qualities pass away if you take your attention from them; because your attention is the sap of life which sustains the expression of your life.

~~~~~~~~~

Subjective words . . subconscious assumptions . . awaken what they affirm.

They are living and active and

*"shall not return unto me void,
but shall accomplish that which I please,
and shall prosper in the thing whereto I sent them."*

They are endowed with the intelligence pertaining to their mission and will persist until the object of their existence is realized; they persist until they awaken the vibratory correlates of themselves, within the one toward whom they are directed, but the moment the object of their creation is accomplished they cease to be.

The word spoken subjectively in quiet confidence will always awaken a corresponding state in the one in whom it was spoken; but the moment its task is accomplished it ceases to be, permitting the one in whom the state is realized to remain in the consciousness of the state affirmed or to return to his former state.

Whatever state has your attention holds your life. Therefore, to become attentive to a former state is to return to that condition.

"Remember not the former things, neither consider things of old."

Nothing can be added to man, for the whole of creation is already perfected in him.

"The kingdom of heaven is within you."

"Man can receive nothing, except it be given him from heaven."

~~~~~~~~~

"I AM the Lord thy God who led thee out of the land of darkness; out of the house of bondage."

I AM, your awareness, is Lord and Master and besides your awareness there is neither Lord nor Master. You are Master of all that you will ever be aware of being.

You know that you are, do you not?

Knowing that you are is the Lord and Master of that which you know that you are.

You could be completely isolated by man from that which you are conscious of being; yet you would, in spite of all human barriers, effortlessly draw to yourself all that you were conscious of being.

The man who is conscious of being poor does not need the assistance of anyone to express his poverty. The man who is conscious of being sick, though isolated in the most hermetically sealed germ-proof area in the world, would express sickness.

There is no barrier to God, for God is your awareness of being.

Regardless of what you are aware of being, you can and do express it without effort.

Stop looking for the Master to come; he is with you always. *"I AM with you always, even unto the end of the world."*

~~~~~~~~~

As *"the worlds were framed by the Word of God"*, so we as

"imitators of God as dear children"

create the conditions and circumstances of our lives by our all-powerful human inner words.

Without practice, the most profound knowledge of the game would produce no desired results.

"To him that knoweth to do good"

that is, knoweth the rules, and doeth it not, to him it is sin.

In other words, he will miss his mark and fail to realize his goal.

In the parable of the Talents, the Master's condemnation of the servant who neglected to use his gift is clear and unmistakable, and having discovered one of the rules of the game of life, we risk failure by ignoring it.

The talent not used, like the limb not exercised, slumbers and finally atrophies. We must be

"doers of the Word, and not hearers only".

Since thinking follows the tracks laid down in one's own inner conversations, not only can we see where we are going on the playing field of life by observing our inner conversations, but also, we can determine where we will go by controlling and directing our inner talking.

What would you think and say and do were you already the one you want to be? Begin to think and say and do this inwardly. You are told that

> "there is a rod in heaven that revealeth secrets,"

and, you must always remember that heaven is within you; and to make it crystal clear who God is, where He is, and what His secrets are,

> Daniel continues,
>
> "Thy dream, and the visions of thy head are these".

They reveal the tracks to which you are tied, and point the direction in which you are going.

~~~~~~~~~

The inner world was as real to Blake as the outer land of waking life.

He looked upon his dreams and visions as the realities of the forms of nature. Blake reduced everything to the bedrock of his own consciousness.

> "The Kingdom of Heaven is within you."

The Real Man, the Imaginative Man, has invested the outer world with all of its properties. The apparent reality of the outer world which is so hard to dissolve is only proof of the absolute reality of the inner world of his own imagination.

> "No man can come to me,
> except the Father which hath
> sent me draw him...
> I and My Father are One."

The world which is described from observation is a manifestation of the mental activity of the observer.

When man discovers that his world is his own mental activity made visible, that no man can come unto him except he draws him, and that there is no one to change but himself, his own imaginative self, his first impulse is to reshape the world in the image of his ideal.

But his ideal is not so easily incarnated. In that moment when he ceases to conform to external discipline, he must impose upon himself a far more rigorous discipline, the self-discipline upon which the realization of his ideal depends.

Imagination is not entirely untrammeled and free to move at will without any rules to constrain it. In fact, the contrary is true. Imagination travels according to habit. Imagination has choice, but it chooses according to habit.

Awake or asleep, man's imagination is constrained to follow certain definite patterns. It is this benumbing influence of habit that man must change; if he does not, his dreams will fade under the paralysis of custom.

Imagination, which is Christ in man, is not subject to the necessity to produce only that which is perfect and good. It exercises its absolute freedom from necessity by endowing the outer physical self with free will to choose to follow good or evil, order or disorder.

"Choose this day whom ye will serve."

But after the choice is made and accepted, so that it forms the individual's habitual consciousness, then imagination manifests its infinite power and wisdom by molding the outer sensuous world of becoming in the image of the habitual inner speech and actions of the individual.

Neville Goddard's Interpretation of Scripture

It is said,

"You believe in God. Believe also in me for I AM he."

Have the faith of God.

"He made himself one with God and found it not robbery to do the works of God."

Go you and do likewise. Yes, begin to believe your awareness, your consciousness of being to be God. Claim for yourself all the attributes that you have heretofore given an external God and you will begin to express these claims.

~~~~~~~~~

***"For I am not a God afar off.
I AM nearer than your hands and feet,
nearer than your very breathing."***

I AM your awareness of being. I AM that in which all that I shall ever be aware of being shall begin and end.

*"For before the world was I AM;
and when the world shall cease to be, I AM;
before Abraham was, I AM."*

This I AM is your awareness.

"Except the Lord build the house they labor in vain that build it."

'The Lord,' being your consciousness, except that which you seek is first established in your consciousness, you will labor in vain to find it.

All things must begin and end in consciousness.

So, blessed indeed is the man that trusteth in himself . . for man's faith in God will ever be measured by his confidence in himself.

> *"You believe in a God, believe also in me."*

Put not your trust in men for men but reflect the being that you are, and can only bring to you or do unto you that which you have first done unto yourself.

~~~~~~~~~

There are no Ascended Masters. Banish this superstition.

You will forever rise from one level of consciousness (master) to another; in so doing, you manifest the ascended level, expressing this newly acquired consciousness.

Consciousness being Lord and Master, you are the Master Magician conjuring that which you are now conscious of being.

> *"For God (consciousness) calleth those things which be not as though they were":*

Things that are not now seen will be seen the moment you become conscious of being that which is not now seen.

This rising from one level of consciousness to another is the only ascension that you will ever experience. No man can lift you to the level you desire. The power to ascend is within yourself; it is your consciousness.

You appropriate the consciousness of the level you desire to express by claiming that you are now expressing such a level.

This is the ascension. It is limitless, for you will never exhaust your capacity to ascend.

Turn from the human superstition of ascension with its belief in masters, and find the only and everlasting master within yourself.

"Far greater is he that is in you than he that is in the world."

Believe this. Do not continue in blindness, following after the mirage of masters. I assure you, your search can end only in disappointment.

~~~~~~~~

"No man taketh away my life, I lay it down myself."

I have the power to lay it down and the power to take it up again.

No matter what happens to man in this world it is never an accident. It occurs under the guidance of an exact and changeless Law.

"No man" (manifestation) "comes unto me except the father within me draw him,"

and

"I and my father are one."

Believe this truth and you will be free. Man has always blamed others for that which he is and will continue to do so until he finds himself as cause of all.

~~~~~~~~

Neville Goddard's Interpretation of Scripture

Jesus, in stating that,

"He and His Father were one but that His Father was greater than He",

revealed His awareness (Father) to be one with that which He was aware of being. He found Himself as Father or awareness to be greater than that which He as Jesus was aware of being.

You and your conception of yourself are one. You are and always will be greater than any conception you will ever have of yourself.

Man fails to do the works of Jesus Christ because he attempts to accomplish them from his present level of consciousness.

You will never transcend your present accomplishments through sacrifice and struggle. Your present level of consciousness will only be transcended as you drop the present state and rise to a higher level.

You rise to a higher level of consciousness by taking your attention away from your present limitations and placing it upon that which you desire to be.

Do not attempt this in day-dreaming or wishful thinking, but in a positive manner. Claim yourself to be the thing desired. I AM that; no sacrifice, no diet, no human tricks.

All that is asked of you is to accept your desire. If you dare claim it, you will express it.

~~~~~~~~~

I AM" comes not to destroy but to fulfill.

"I AM," the awareness within you, destroys nothing but ever fill full the molds or conception one has of one's self.

It is impossible for the poor man to find wealth in this world no matter how he is surrounded with it until he first claims himself to be wealthy.

For signs follow, they do not precede.

To constantly kick and complain against the limitations of poverty while remaining poor in consciousness is to play the fool's game. Changes cannot take place from that level of consciousness for life in constantly out picturing all levels.

Follow the example of the prodigal son. Realize that you, yourself brought about this condition of waste and lack and make the decision within yourself to rise to a higher level where the fatted calf, the ring, and the robe await your claim.

There was no condemnation of the prodigal when he had the courage to claim this inheritance as his own. Others will condemn us only as long as we continue in that for which we condemn ourselves.

~~~~~~~~

"Ye shall know the truth, and the truth shall make you free."

Men claim that a true judgment must conform to the external reality to which it relates.

This means that if I, while imprisoned, suggest to myself that I am free and succeed in believing that I am free, it is true that I believe in my freedom; but it does not follow that I am free, for I may be the victim of illusion.

But, because of my own experiences, I have come to believe in so many strange things that I see little reason to doubt the truth of things that are beyond my experience.

The ancient teachers warned us not to judge from appearances because, said they, the truth need not conform to the external reality to which it relates.

They claimed that we bore false witness if we imagined evil against another, that no matter how real our belief appears to be, how truly it conforms to the external reality to which it relates, if it does not make free, the one of whom we hold the belief, it is untrue and therefore a false judgment.

We are called upon to deny the evidence of our senses and to imagine as true of our neighbor that which makes him free.

"Ye shall know the truth, and the truth shall make you free."

To know the truth of our neighbor we must assume that he is already that which he desires to be. Any concept we hold of another that is short of his fulfilled desire, will not make him free and therefore cannot be the truth.

~~~~~~~~~~

"I know and am persuaded by the Lord Jesus that there is nothing unclean of itself, but to him that esteemeth anything to be unclean, to him it is unclean."

Stop asking yourself whether you are worthy or unworthy to receive that which you desire. You, as man, did not create the desire. Your desires are ever fashioned within you because of what you now claim yourself to be.

When a man is hungry, (without thinking) he automatically desires food. When imprisoned, he automatically desires freedom and so forth.

Your desires contain within themselves the plan of self-expression.

So leave all judgments out of the picture and rise in consciousness to the level of your desire and make yourself one with it by claiming it to be so now.

~~~~~~~~

"Leave all and follow Me"

is a double invitation to you.

First, it invites you to turn completely away from all problems and, then, it calls upon you to continue walking in the claim that you are that which you desire to be.

Do not be a Lot's wife who looks back and becomes salted or preserved in the dead past. Be a Lot who does not look back but who keeps his vision focused upon the promised land, the thing desired.

Do this and you will know that you have found the master, the Master Magician, making the unseen the seen,

through the command,

"I AM THAT"

~~~~~~~~

"My grace is sufficient for thee. My strength is made perfect in weakness."

Have faith in this unseen claim until the conviction is born within you that it is so. Your confidence in this claim will pay great rewards.

Just a little while and he, the thing desired, will come. But without faith it is impossible to realize anything. Through faith the worlds were framed because

> *"faith is the substance of the thing hoped for, the evidence of the thing not yet seen."*

Don't be anxious or concerned as to results. They will follow just as surely as day follows night.

Look upon your desires, all of them, as the spoken words of God, and every word or desire a promise.

The reason most of us fail to realize our desires is because we are constantly conditioning them. Do not condition your desire. Just accept it as it comes to you. Give thanks for it to the point that you are grateful for having already received it, then go about your way in peace.

Such acceptance of your desire is like dropping seed, fertile seed, into prepared soil.

For when you can drop the thing desired in consciousness, confident that it shall appear, you have done all that is expected to you.

But, to be worried or concerned about the how of your desire maturing is to hold these fertile seeds in a mental grasp, and, therefore, never to have dropped them in the soil of confidence.

The reason men condition their desires is because they constantly judge after the appearance of being and see the things as real, forgetting that the only reality is the consciousness back of them.

To see things as real, is to deny that all things are possible to God (consciousness). The man who is imprisoned and sees his four walls as real is automatically denying the urge or promise of God within him of freedom.

~~~~~~~~~

Life is no respecter of persons and destroys nothing, it continues to keep alive that which he is conscious of being.

Things will disappear only as man changes in consciousness.

Deny it if you will, it still remains a fact that consciousness is the only reality and things but mirror that which you are in consciousness. So the heavenly state you are seeking will be found only in consciousness, for the kingdom of heaven is within you.

As the will of heaven is ever done on earth, you are today living in the heaven, that you have established within you. For here on this very earth, your heaven, reveals itself.

The kingdom of heaven really is at hand. now is the accepted time. So create a new heaven, enter into a new state of consciousness and a new earth will appear.

> "The former things shall pass away. They shall not be remembered not come into mind any more. For behold, I," (your consciousness) "come quickly and my reward is with me."

I AM nameless but will take upon myself every name (nature) that you call me.

Remember it is you, yourself, that I speak of as 'me.' So every conception that you have of yourself, that is every deep conviction, you have of yourself is that which you shall appear as being,

>for I AM not fooled;

>"God is not mocked."

~~~~~~~~~

"But whom say ye that I AM?"

>"I AM the Lord; that is My name;
>and My glory will I not give to another."

>"I AM the Lord, the God of all Flesh."

This I AM within you, the reader, this awareness, this consciousness of being, is the Lord, the God of all Flesh.

I AM is He that should come; stop looking for another.

As long as you believe in a God apart from yourself, you will continue to transfer the power of your expression to your conceptions, forgetting that you are the conceiver.

The power conceiving and the thing conceived are one but the power to conceive is greater than the conception. Jesus discovered this glorious truth when He declared,

>"I and My Father are one, but My Father is greater than I."

The power conceiving itself to be man is greater than its conception. All conceptions are limitations of the conceiver.

~~~~~~~~~

". . . be ye therefore wise as serpents, and harmless as doves."

The serpent's ability to form its skin by ossifying a portion of itself, and its skill in shedding each skin as it outgrew it, caused man to regard this reptile as a symbol of the power of endless growth and self-reproduction.

Man is told, therefore, to be

"wise as the serpent"

and learn how to shed his skin, his environment, which is his solidified self; man must learn how to

"loose him, and let him go"

. . how to

"put off the old man" . . .

how to die to the old and yet know, like the serpent, that he

"shall not surely die".

Man has not learned as yet that all that is outside his physical body is also a part of himself, that his world and all the conditions of his life are but the out picturing of his state of consciousness.

When he knows this truth, he will stop the futile struggle of self-contention and, like the serpent, let the old go and grow a new environment.

> "Man is immortal; therefore he must
> die endlessly. For life is a creative idea;
> it can only find itself in changing forms."
> . . . Tagore

In ancient times, serpents were also associated with the guardianship of treasure or wealth.

The injunction to be

"wise as serpents"

is the advice to man to awaken the power of his subtilized body, his imagination, that he, like the serpent, may grow and outgrow, die and yet not die, for from such deaths and resurrections alone, shedding the old and putting on the new, shall come fulfillment of his dreams and the finding of his treasures.

As

"the serpent was more subtle than any beast of the field which the Lord God had made"

even so, imagination is more subtle than any creature of the heavens which the Lord God had created.

Imagination is the creature that:"

. . .was made subject to vanity, not willingly, but by reason of him who hath subjected the same in hope. . .For we are saved by hope: but hope that is seen is not hope: for what a man seeth, why doth he yet hope for it? But if we hope for that we see not, then do we have patience wait for it."

Although the outer, or "natural", man of the senses is interlocked with his environment, the inner, or spiritual, man of imagination is not thus interlocked. If the interlocking were complete, the charge to be

"wise as serpents"

would be in vain. Were we completely interlocked with our environment, we could not withdraw our attention from the evidence of the senses and feel ourselves into the situation of our fulfilled desire, in hope that that unseen state would solidify as our new environment.

~~~~~~~~~

Another story is told us; of the widow and the three drops of oil.

The prophet asked the widow,

"What have ye in your house?"

And she replied,

"Three drops of oil."

He then said to her,

"Go borrow vessels. Close the door after ye have returned into your house and begin to pour."

And she poured from three drops of oil into all the borrowed vessels, filling them to capacity with oil remaining.

You, the reader, are this widow. You have not a husband to impregnate you or make you fruitful, for a 'widow' is a barren state.

Your awareness is now the Lord, or the prophet that has become your husband. Follow the example of the widow, who instead of recognizing an emptiness or nothingness, recognized the something, three drops of oil.

Then the command to her,

"Go within and close the door,"

that is, shut the door of the senses that tell you of the empty measures, the debts, the problems. When you have taken your attention away completely by shutting out the evidence of the senses, begin to feel the joy, (symbolized by oil), of having received the things desired.

When the agreement is established within you so that all doubts and fears have passed away, then, you too will fill all the empty measures of your life and will have an abundance running over.

Recognition is the power that conjures in the world. Every state that you have ever recognized, you have embodied.

That which you are recognizing as true of yourself today is that which you are experiencing.

So be as the widow and recognize joy, no matter how little the beginnings of recognition, and you will be generously rewarded, for the world is a magnified mirror, magnifying everything that you are conscious of being.

~~~~~~~~~

**"I AM the Lord the God, which has brought thee out of the land of Egypt,
out of the house of bondage;
thou shalt have no other gods before me."**

What a glorious revelation, your awareness, now revealed as the Lord thy God!

Come, awake from your dream of being imprisoned.

Realize that the earth is yours,

"and the fullness thereof; the world, and all that dwells therein."

You have become so enmeshed in the belief that you are man that you have forgotten the glorious being that you are.

Now with your memory restored decree the unseen to appear, and it shall appear, for all things are compelled to respond to the Voice of God, Your awareness of being.

The world is AT YOUR COMMAND

~~~~~~~~

"Before Abraham was, I AM." Before the world was, I AM.

Consciousness precedes all manifestations and is the prop upon which all manifestation rests. To remove the manifestations, all that is required of you, the conceiver, is to take your attention away from the conception.

Instead of "Out of sight, out of mind", it really is "Out of mind, out of sight".

The manifestation will remain in sight only as long as it takes the force with which the conceiver, "I AM", originally endowed it to spend itself. This applies to all creation from the infinitesimally small electron to the infinitely great universe.

~~~~~~~~

Neville Goddard's Interpretation of Scripture

"Verily, verily, I say unto you, before Abraham was, I AM."

"In the beginning was the Word, and the Word was with God, and the Word was God"

In the beginning was the unconditioned awareness of being, and the unconditioned awareness of being became conditioned by imagining itself to be something, and the unconditioned awareness of being became that which it had imagined itself to be; so did creation begin.

By this law, first conceiving, then becoming that conceived, all things evolve out of nothing; and without this sequence there is not anything made that is made.

~~~~~~~~~

"I can of mine own self do nothing."

Since creation is finished, it is impossible to force anything into being.

The example of magnetism previously given is a good illustration. You cannot make magnetism; it can only be displayed. You cannot make the law of magnetism.

If you want to build a magnet, you can do so only by conforming to the law of magnetism. In other words, you surrender yourself, or yield to the law. In like manner, when you use the faculty of assumption, you are conforming to a law just as real as the law governing magnetism.

You can neither create nor change the law of assumption.

It is in this respect that you are impotent. You can only yield or conform, and since all of your experiences are the result of your assumptions, consciously or unconsciously, the value of consciously using the power of assumption surely must be obvious.

Willingly identify yourself with that which you most desire, knowing that it will find expression through you.

Yield to the feeling of the wish fulfilled and be consumed as its victim, then rise as the prophet of the law of assumption.

~~~~~~~~~

"There is a natural body, and there is a spiritual body."

The spiritual body of imagination is not interlocked with man's environment. The spiritual body can withdraw from the outer man of sense and environment and imagine itself to be what it wants to be.

And if it remains faithful to the vision, imagination will build for man a new environment in which to live. This is what is meant by the statement:

> "...I go to prepare a place for you.
> And if I go and prepare a place for you,
> I will come again, and receive you unto
> myself; that where I am, there ye may be also."

The place that is prepared for you need not be a place in space. It can be health, wealth, companionship, anything that you desire in this world. Now, how is the place prepared?

You must first construct as life-like a representation as possible of what you would see and hear and do if you were physically present and physically moving about in that "place."

Then, with your physical body immobilized, you must imagine that you are actually in that "place" and are seeing and hearing and doing all that you would see and hear and do if you were there physically.

This you must do over and over again until it takes on the tones of reality. When it feels natural, the "place" has been prepared as the new environment for your outer or physical self. Now you may open your physical eyes and return to your former state.

The "place" is prepared, and where you have been in imagination, there you shall be in the body also.

How this imagined state is realized physically is not the concern of you, the natural or outer man.

The spiritual body, on its return from the imagined state to its former physical state, created an invisible bridge of incident to link the two states. Although the curious feeling that you were actually there and that the state was real is gone, as soon as you open your eyes upon the old familiar environment, nevertheless, you are haunted with the sense of a double identity, with the knowledge that "there is a natural body, and there is a spiritual body."

When you, the natural man, have had this experience you will go automatically across the bridge of events which leads to the physical realization of your invisibly prepared place.

This concept, that man is dual and that the inner man of imagination can dwell in future states and return to the present moment with a bridge of events to link the two, clashes violently with the widely accepted view about the human personality and the cause and nature of phenomena.

Such a concept demands a revolution in current ideas about the human personality, and about space, time and matter.

The concept that man, consciously or unconsciously, determines the conditions of life by imagining himself into these mental states, leads to the conclusion that this supposedly solid world is a construction of Mind, a concept which, at first, common sense rejects.

However, we should remember that most of the concepts which common sense at first rejected, man was afterward forced to accept. These never-ending reversals of judgment which experience has forced upon man led Professor Whitehead to write:

> "Heaven knows what seeming nonsense may not tomorrow be demonstrated truth."

> The creative power in man sleeps and needs to be awakened.

> "Awake thou that sleepest, and arise from the dead."

Wake from the sleep that tells you the outer world is the cause of the conditions of your life. Rise from the dead past and create a new environment.

~~~~~~~~~

"Before Abraham or the world was, I AM."

"When all of time shall cease to be, I AM."

I AM the formless awareness of being conceiving myself to be man. By my everlasting law of being I AM compelled to be and to express all that I believe myself to be.

I AM the eternal Nothingness containing within my formless self the capacity to be all things. I AM that in which all my conceptions of myself live and move and have their being, and apart from which they are not.

I dwell within every conception of myself; from this withinness, I ever seek to transcend all conceptions of myself. By the very law of my being, I transcend my conceptions of myself, only as I believe myself to be that which does transcend.

I AM the law of being and beside ME there is no law.

I AM that I AM.

~~~~~~~~~

"Be still and know that I AM God."

Yes, this very I AM, your awareness of being, is God, the only God.

I AM is the Lord, the God of all Flesh, all manifestation.

This presence, your unconditioned awareness, comprehends neither beginning nor ending; limitations exist only in the manifestation.

When you realize that this awareness is your eternal self, you will know that before Abraham was, I AM.

~~~~~~~~~

"What think ye of the Christ?

Whose Son is He?"

"When this question is asked of you, let your answer be,

Neville Goddard's Interpretation of Scripture

"Christ is my imagination",

*"and, though I See not
yet all things put under him,"*

yet I know that I am Mary from whom sooner or later He shall be born, and eventually

"Do all things through Christ."

The birth of Christ is the awakening of the inner or Second man. It is becoming conscious of the mental activity within oneself, which activity continues whether we are conscious of it or not.

The birth of Christ does not bring any person from a distance, or make anything to be that was not there before.

It is the unveiling of the Son of God in man.

The Lord

"cometh in clouds"

is the prophet's description of the pulsating rings of golden liquid light on the head of him in whom He awakes. The coming is from within and not from without, as Christ is in us.

This great mystery, God was manifest in the flesh, begins with Advent, and it is appropriate that the cleansing of the Temple,

"Which temple ye are,"

stands in the forefront of the Christian mysteries.

"The Kingdom of Heaven is within you."

Advent is unveiling the mystery of your being.

If you will practice the art of revision by a life lived according to the wise, imaginative use of your inner speech and inner actions, in confidence that by the conscious use of

"the power that worketh in us",

Christ will awake in you; if you believe it, trust it, act upon it;

Christ will awake in you.

This is Advent.

"Great is the mystery, God was manifest in the flesh."

From Advent on,

"He that toucheth you toucheth the apple of God's eye."

~~~~~~~~~

Whatever you desire is already

"furnished and prepared".

Your imagination can put you in touch inwardly with that state of consciousness. If you imagine that you are already the one you want to be,

you are following the

"man bearing a pitcher of water".

If you remain in that state, you have entered the guest-chamber . . Passover . . and committed your spirit into the hands of God . . your consciousness.

Neville Goddard's Interpretation of Scripture

A man's state of consciousness is his demand on the Infinite Store House of God, and, like the law of commerce, a demand creates a supply.

To change the supply, you change the demand . . your state of consciousness.

What you desire to be, that you must feel you already are. Your state of consciousness creates the conditions of your life, rather than the conditions create your state of consciousness.

To know this Truth, is to have the

"water of life".

But your savior . . the solution of your problem . . cannot be manifested by such knowledge only.

It can be realized only as such knowledge is applied.

Only as you assume the feeling of your wish fulfilled, and continue therein, is your side pierced;

"from whence cometh blood and water".

In this manner only is Jesus, the solution of your problem, realized.

~~~~~~~~~

"In Him we live and move, and have our being."

Psychically, this world appears as an ocean of light containing within itself all things, including man, as pulsating bodies enveloped in liquid light.

The Biblical story of the Flood is the state in which man lives. Man is actually inundated in an ocean of liquid light in which countless numbers of light-beings move.

The story of the Flood is really being enacted today. Man is the Ark containing within himself the male-female principles of every living thing. The dove or idea which is sent out to find dry land is man's attempt to embody his ideas. Man's ideas resemble birds in flight . . like the dove in the story, returning to man without finding a place to rest.

If man will not let such fruitless searches discourage him, one day the bird will return with a green sprig. After assuming the consciousness of the thing desired, he will be convinced that it is so; and he will feel and know that he is that which he has consciously appropriated, even though it is not yet confirmed by his senses. One day man will become so identified with his conception that he will know it to be himself, and he will declare,

"I AM";

I AM that which I desire to be
"I AM that I AM"

He will find that, as he does so, he will begin to embody his desire (the dove or desire will this time find dry land), thereby realizing the mystery of the word made flesh.

Everything in the world is a crystallization of this liquid light.

"I AM the light of the world"

Your awareness of being is the liquid light of the world, which crystallizes into the conceptions you have of yourself.

Your unconditioned awareness of being first conceived itself in liquid light (which is the initial velocity of the universe).

All things, from the highest to the lowest vibrations or expressions of life, are nothing more than the different vibrations of velocities of this initial velocity; gold, silver, iron, wood, flesh etc., are only different expressions or velocities of this one substance-liquid light.

All things are crystallized liquid light; the differentiation or infinity of expression is caused by the conceiver's desire to know himself.

Your conception of yourself automatically determines the velocity necessary to express that which you have conceived yourself to be.

The world is an ocean of liquid light in countless different states of crystallization.

~~~~~~~~~

"No man (or manifestation) cometh unto My Father save by Me."

The I AM (your consciousness) is the only door through which anything can pass into your world.

Stop looking for signs. Signs follow; they do not precede. Begin to reverse the statement, "Seeing is believing", to "Believing is seeing".

Start now to believe, not with the wavering confidence based on deceptive external evidence but with an undaunted confidence based on the immutable law that you can be that which you desire to be. You will find that you are not a victim of fate, but a victim of faith (your own).

Only through one door can that which you seek pass into the world of manifestation.

Neville Goddard's Interpretation of Scripture

"I AM the door".

~~~~~~~~~

"Go, tell no man of this holy thing that you have conceived".

Lock your secret within you and magnify the Lord, magnify or believe, your desire to be your savior, coming to be with you.

When this belief is so firmly established that you feel confident of results, your desire will embody itself. How it will be done, no man knows.

I, your desire, have ways ye know not of;
my ways are past finding out.

Your desire can be likened to a seed, and seeds contain within themselves both the power and the plan of self-expression. Your consciousness is the soil.

These seeds are successfully planted only if, after you have claimed yourself to be and to have that which you desire, you confidently await results without an anxious thought.

If I be lifted up in consciousness to the naturalness of my desire, I shall automatically draw the manifestation unto me.

Consciousness is the door through which life reveals itself. Consciousness is always objectifying itself.

To be conscious of being or possessing anything is to be or have that which you are conscious of being or possessing.

Therefore, lift yourself to the consciousness of your desire and you will see it automatically out picture itself.

"Salute no man on the highway"

See no man as an authority.

Why should you ask man for permission to express, when you realize that your world, in its every detail, originated within you and is sustained by you as the only conceptional center?

Your whole world may be likened to solidified space mirroring the beliefs and acceptances as projected by a formless, faceless presence, namely, I AM.

Reduce the whole to its primordial substance and nothing would remain but you, a dimensionless presence, the conceiver.

The conceiver is a law apart. Conceptions under such law are not to be measured by past accomplishments or modified by present capacities for, without taking thought, the conception in a way unknown to man expresses itself.

Go within secretly and appropriate the new consciousness. Feel yourself to be it, and the former limitations shall pass away as completely and as easily as snow on a hot summer's day. You will not even remember the former limitations; they were never part of this new consciousness.

~~~~~~~~~~

This rebirth Jesus referred to, when he said to Nicodemus,

"Ye must be born again,"

was nothing more than moving from one state of consciousness to another.

"Whatsoever ye shall ask in My name, that will I do."

This certainly does not mean to ask in words, pronouncing with the lips the sounds, God or Christ Jesus, for millions have asked in this manner without results.

To feel yourself to be a thing is to have asked for that thing in His name. I AM is the nameless presence. To feel yourself to be rich is to ask for wealth in His name.

I AM is unconditioned. It is neither rich nor poor, strong nor weak. In other words, in him there is neither Greek nor Jew, bond nor free, male nor female.

These are all conceptions or limitations of the limitless, and therefore names of the nameless.

To feel yourself to be anything is to ask the nameless,
I AM,

to express that name or nature".

"Ask whatsoever ye will in My name
by appropriating the nature of the thing desired
and I will give it unto you".

~~~~~~~~~

The rules governing the game of life are simple, but it takes a lifetime of practice to use them wisely.

Here is one of the rules:

"As he thinketh in his heart, so is he."

Thinking is usually believed to be a function entirely untrammeled and free, without any rules to constrain it. But that is not true. Thinking moves by its own processes in a bounded territory, with definite paths and patterns.

> "Thinking follows the tracks
> laid down in one's own inner
> conversations."

All of us can realize our objectives by the wise use of mind and speech.

Most of us are totally unaware of the mental activity which goes on within us. But to play the game of life successfully, we must become aware of our every mental activity, for this activity, in the form of inner conversations, is the cause of the outer phenomena of our life.

> ". . . *every idle word that man shall speak,*
> *they shall give account thereof in the day of judgment.*
> *For by thy words thou shall be justified,*
> *and by thy words thou shalt be condemned.*"

The law of the Word cannot be broken.

> ". . .*A bone of him shall not be broken.*"

The law of the Word never overlooks an inner word nor makes the smallest allowance for our ignorance of its power. It fashions life about us as we, by our inner conversations, fashion life within ourselves. This is done to reveal to us our position on the playing field of life. There is no opponent in the game of life; there is only the goal.

~~~~~~~~~

When Jesus discovered His consciousness to be this wonderful law of self-government,

He declared,

"And now I sanctify Myself that they also might be sanctified through the truth."

He knew that consciousness was the only reality, that things objectified, were nothing more than different states of consciousness. Jesus warned His followers to seek first the Kingdom of Heaven (that state of consciousness that would produce the thing desired) and all things would be added to them.

He also stated, *"I AM the truth."*

He knew that man's consciousness was the truth or cause of all that man saw his world to be.

Jesus realized that the world was made in the likeness of man. He knew that man saw his world to be what it was because man was what he was. In short, man's conception of himself determines that which he sees his world to be.

~~~~~~~~~

"All things are made by God (consciousness) and without him there is nothing made that is made."

Creation is judged good and very good because it is the perfect likeness of that consciousness which produced it.

To be conscious of being one thing and then see yourself expressing something other than that which you are conscious of being is a violation of the law of being; therefore, it would not be good.

The law of being is never broken; man ever sees himself expressing that which he is conscious of being. Be it good, bad or indifferent, it is nevertheless a perfect likeness of his conception of himself; it is good and very good.

Not only are all things made by God, all things are made of God. All are the offspring of God. God is one. Things or divisions are the projections of the one.

God being one, He must command Himself to be the seeming other for there is no other.

The absolute cannot contain something within itself that is not itself. If it did, then it would not be absolute, the only one.

~~~~~~~~

Commands, to be effective, must be to oneself.

"I AM that I AM"

is the only effective command.

"I AM the Lord and beside Me there is none else."

You cannot command that which is not. As there is no other, you must command yourself to be that which you would have appear.

Let me clarify what I mean by effective command. You do not repeat like a parrot the statement,

"I AM that I AM";

such vain repetition would be both stupid and fruitless.

It is not the words that make it effective; it is the consciousness of being the thing which makes it effective.

When you say, "I AM", you are declaring yourself to be.

The word 'that' in the statement, "I AM that I AM", indicates that which you would be.

The second "I AM" in the quotation is the cry of victory.

This whole drama takes place inwardly with or without the use of words.

~~~~~~~~~

"Be still and know that you are".

This stillness is attained by observing the observer. Repeat quietly but with feeling, "I AM . . I AM", until you have lost all consciousness of the world and know yourself just as being.

Awareness, the knowing that you are, is Almighty God; I AM.

After this is accomplished, define yourself as that which you desire to be by feeling yourself to be the thing desired:

"I AM that."

This understanding that you are the thing desired will cause a thrill to course through your entire being. When the conviction is established and you really believe that you are that which you desired to be, then the second "I AM" is uttered as a cry of victory.

This mystical revelation of Moses can be seen as three distinct steps:

I AM;

I AM free;

I really AM!

It does not matter what the appearances round about you are like.

"All things make way for the coming of the Lord."

I AM the Lord coming in the appearance of that which I AM conscious of being.

All the inhabitants of the earth cannot stay my coming or question my authority, to be, that which I AM conscious that I AM

~~~~~~~~~

Righteousness is defined as the consciousness of already being what you want to be.

This is the true psychological meaning and obviously does not refer to adherence to moral codes, civil law or religious precepts.

You cannot attach too much importance to being righteous. In fact, the entire Bible is permeated with admonition and exhortations on this subject.

"Break off thy sins by righteousness."

"My righteousness I hold fast, and will not let it go: my heart shall not reproach me so long as I live."

"My righteousness shall answer for me

in time to come."

Very often the words sin and righteousness are used in the same quotation. This is a logical contrast of opposites and becomes enormously significant in the light of the psychological meaning of righteousness and the psychological meaning of sin.

Sin means to miss the mark. Not to attain your desire, not to be the person you want to be is sinning.

Righteousness is the consciousness of already being what you want to be.

It is a changeless educative law that effects must follow causes.

Only by righteousness can you be saved from sinning.

~~~~~~~~~

"I AM the light of the world,"

crystallizing into the form of my conception of myself.

Consciousness is the eternal light, which crystallizes only through the medium of your conception of yourself. Change your conception of yourself and you will automatically change the world in which you live.

Do not try to change people; they are only messengers telling you who you are. Revalue yourself and they will confirm the change.

Now you will realize why Jesus sanctified Himself instead of others, why to the pure all things are pure, why in Christ Jesus (the awakened consciousness) there is no condemnation. Awake from the sleep of condemnation and prove the principle of life. Stop not only your judgment of others but your condemnation of yourself.

~~~~~~~~

Hear the revelation of the enlightened,

"I know and am persuaded by the Lord Christ Jesus that there is nothing unclean of itself, but to him that seeth anything to be unclean to him it is unclean,"

and again,

"Happy is the man who condemneth himself not in that which he alloweth."

Stop asking yourself whether or not you are worthy or unworthy to claim yourself to be that which you desire to be. You will be condemned by the world only as long as you condemn yourself.

You do not need to work out anything.
The works are finished.

The principle by which all things are made and without which there is not anything made that is made, is eternal.

You are this principle.

Your awareness of being is this everlasting law.

You have never expressed anything that you were not aware of being and you never will.

Assume the consciousness of that which you desire to express. Claim it, until it becomes a natural manifestation. Feel it and live within that feeling, until you make it your nature.

Neville Goddard's Interpretation of Scripture

~~~~~~~~~

"Then the LORD God formed man of dust from the ground, and breathed into his nostrils the breath of life; and man became a living being."

"As thou knowest not what is the way of the spirit, nor how the bones do grow in the womb of her that is with child: even so thou knowest not the works of God who maketh all/ Just as you don't know how the breath of life enters the limbs of a child within its mother's womb, you also don't understand how God, who made everything, works."

"And it came to pass after these things, that the son of the woman, the mistress of the house, fell sick; and his sickness was so sore, that there was no breath left in him."

"And he (Elisha) went up, and lay upon the child, and put his mouth upon his mouth, and his eyes upon his eyes, and his hands upon his hands: and stretched himself upon the child; and the flesh of the child waxed warm."

"But after the three and a half days, the breath of life from God came into them, and they stood on their feet; and great fear fell upon those who were watching them."

Did the Prophet Elijah really restore to life the dead child of the Widow?

This story, along with all the other stories of the Bible, is a psychological drama which takes place in the consciousness of man.

The Widow symbolizes every man and woman in the world; the dead child represents the frustrated desires and ambitions of man; while the prophet, Elijah, symbolizes the God power within man, or man's awareness of being.

The story tells us that the prophet took the dead child from the Widow's bosom and carried him into an upper room. As he entered this upper room he closed the door behind them; placing the child upon a bed, he breathed life into him; returning to the mother, he gave her the child and said,

"Woman, thy son liveth"

Man's desires can be symbolized as the dead child. The mere fact that he desires, is positive proof that the thing desired is not yet a living reality in his world. He tries in every conceivable way to nurse this desire into reality, to make it live, but finds in the end that all attempts are fruitless.

Most men are not aware of the existence of the infinite power within themselves as the prophet.

They remain indefinitely with a dead child in their arms, not realizing that the desire is the positive indication of limitless capacities for its fulfillment.

Let man once recognize that his consciousness is a prophet who breathes life into all that he is conscious of being, and he will close the door of his senses against his problem and fix his attention, solely on that which he desires, knowing that by so doing, his desires are certain to be realized.

He will discover recognition to be the breath of life, for he will perceive, as he consciously claims himself to be now expressing or possessing all he desires to be or to have, that he will be breathing the breath of life into his desire. The quality claimed for the desire (in a way unknown to him) will begin to move and become a living reality in his world.

Yes, the Prophet Elijah lives forever as man's limitless consciousness of being, the widow as his limited consciousness of being and the child as that which he desires to be.

Listen carefully to the promise,

*"Ye shall not need to fight in this battle:
Set yourself, stand still, and see the
salvation of the Lord with you."*

With you!

That particular consciousness with which you are identified is the Lord of the agreement. He will without assistance establish the thing agreed upon on earth.

Can you, in the face of the army of reasons why a thing cannot be done, quietly enter into an agreement with the Lord that it is done?

Can you, now that you have found the Lord to be your awareness of being, become aware that the battle is won? Can you, no matter how near and threatening the enemy seems to be, continue in your confidence, standing still, knowing that the victory is yours?

If you can, you will see the salvation of the Lord.

~~~~~~~~~

"Not My will, but Thine, be done."

This resignation is not one of blind realization that

*"I can of Myself do nothing,
the Father within Me,
He doeth the work"*

When man wills, he attempts to make something which does not now exist appear in time and space. Too often we are not aware of that which we are really doing. We unconsciously state that we do not possess the capacities to express. We predicate our desire upon the hope of acquiring the necessary capacities in future time.

"I AM not, but I will be".

Man does not realize that consciousness is the Father which does the work, so he attempts to express that which he is not conscious of being.

Such struggles are doomed to failure; only the present expresses itself. Unless I am conscious of being that which I seek, I will not find it.

God (your awareness) is the substance and fullness of all.

God's will is the recognition of that which is, not of that which will be.

Instead of seeing this saying as

"Thine will be done",

see it as

"Thy will is done".

The works are finished.

~~~~~~~~

Man becomes what he imagines.

He has a self-determined history. Imagination is the way, the truth, the life revealed. We cannot get hold of truth

with the logical mind. Where the natural man of sense sees a bud, imagination sees a rose full-blown.

Truth cannot be encompassed by facts. As we awaken to the imaginative life, we discover that to imagine a thing is to make it so, that a true judgment need not conform to the external reality to which it relates.

The imaginative man does not deny the reality of the sensuous outer world of Becoming, but he knows that it is the inner world of continuous Imagination that is the force by which the sensuous outer world of Becoming is brought to pass.

He sees the outer world and all its happenings as projections of the inner world of Imagination. To him, everything is a manifestation of the mental activity which goes on in man's imagination, without the sensuous reasonable man being aware of it.

But he realizes that every man must become conscious of this inner activity and see the relationship between the inner causal world of imagination and the sensuous outer world of effects.

It is a marvelous thing to find that you can imagine yourself into the state of your fulfilled desire and escape from the jails which ignorance built.

> The Real Man is a Magnificent Imagination.
>
> It is this self that must be awakened.

"Awake thou that sleepest, and arise from the dead, and Christ shall give thee light."

The moment man discovers that his imagination is Christ, he accomplishes acts which on this level can only be called miraculous.

But until man has the sense of Christ as his imagination,

> *"You did not choose me,*
> *I have chosen you."*

He will see everything in pure objectivity without any subjective relationship.

Not realizing that all that he encounters is part of himself, he rebels at the thought that he has chosen the conditions of his life, that they are related by affinity to his own mental activity.

Man must firmly come to believe that reality lies within him and not without.

Although others have bodies, a life of their own, their reality is rooted in you, ends in you, as yours ends in God.

~~~~~~~~

"Let the weak say,
I AM strong".

Man in his blindness will not heed the prophet's advice; he continues to claim himself to be weak, poor, wretched and all the other undesirable expressions from which he is trying to free himself by ignorantly claiming that he will be free from these characteristics in the expectancy of the future.

Such thoughts thwart the one law that can ever free him.

There is only one door through which that which you seek can enter your world.

"I AM the door."

When you say,

Neville Goddard's Interpretation of Scripture

"I AM",

you are declaring yourself to be, first person, present tense; there is no future. To know that I AM is to be conscious of being. Consciousness is the only door. Unless you are conscious of being that which you seek, you seek in vain.

If you judge after appearances, you will continue to be enslaved by the evidence of your senses.

~~~~~~~~~

"Go within and shut the door"

The door of the senses must be tightly shut before your new claim can be honored. Closing the door of the senses is not as difficult as it appears to be at first. It is done without effort.

It is impossible to serve two masters at the same time.

The master man serves is that which he is conscious of being.

I AM Lord and Master of that which I AM conscious of being. It is no effort for me to conjure poverty if I am conscious of being poor.

My servant (poverty), is compelled to follow me (consciousness of poverty), as long as I AM (the Lord), conscious of being poor.

Instead of fighting against the evidence of the senses, you claim yourself to be that which you desire to be. As your attention is placed on this claim, the doors of the senses automatically close against your former master (that which you were conscious of being).

As you become lost in the feeling of being, that which you are now claiming to be true of yourself, the doors of the senses once more open, revealing your world to be the perfect expression of that which you are conscious of being.

Let us follow the example of Jesus who realized, as man, He could do nothing to change His present picture of lack. He closed the door of His senses against His problem and went to His Father, the one to Whom all things are possible.

Having denied the evidence of His senses, He claimed Himself, to be all that, a moment before, His senses told him, He was not.

Knowing that consciousness expresses its likeness on earth, He remained in the claimed consciousness until the doors (His senses) opened and confirmed the rulership of the Lord.

Remember,

"I AM is Lord of all."

Never again use the will of man which claims,

"I will be".

Be as resigned as Jesus and claim,

"I AM that".

~~~~~~~~~

"He sent his word and healed them, and delivered them from their destructions."

He transmitted the consciousness of health and awoke its vibratory correlate in the one toward whom it was directed.

He mentally represented the subject to himself in a state of health and imagined he heard the subject confirm it.

> *"For no word of God shall be void of power; therefore hold fast the pattern of healthful words which thou has heard."*

To pray successfully you must have clearly defined objectives. You must know what you want before you can ask for it. You must know what you want before you can feel that you have it, and prayer is the feeling of the fulfilled desire.

It does not matter what it is you seek in prayer, or where it is, or whom it concerns.

You have nothing to do but convince yourself of the truth of that which you desire to see manifested.

When you emerge from prayer, you no longer seek, for you have, if you have prayed correctly, subconsciously assumed the reality of the state sought, and by the law of reversibility your subconscious must objectify that which it affirms.

You must have a conductor to transmit a force. You may employ a wire, a jet of water, a current of air, a ray of light or any intermediary whatsoever.

The principle of the photophone or the transmission of the voice by light will help you to understand thought transmission, or the sending of a word to heal another.

There is a strong analogy between a spoken voice and a mental voice. To think is to speak low, to speak is to think aloud.

~~~~~~~~~

There is only one power:

"I AM He."

Because of your belief in external things, you think power into them, by transferring the power that you are, to the external thing.

Realize you, yourself, are the power, you have mistakenly given to outer conditions.

The Bible compares the opinionated man to the camel who could not go through the needle's eye.

The needle's eye referred to was a small gate in the walls of Jerusalem, which was so narrow that a camel could not go through it until relieved of its pack.

The rich man, that is the one burdened with false human concepts, cannot enter the Kingdom of Heaven until relieved of his burden any more than could the camel go through this small gate.

Man feels so secure in his man-made laws, opinions and beliefs that he invests them with an authority they do not possess.

Satisfied that his knowledge is all, he remains unaware that all outward appearances are but states of mind externalized.

When he realizes that the consciousness of a quality externalizes that quality without the aid of any other or many values, and establishes the one true value, his own consciousness.

~~~~~~~~~

> ***"To him that hath (that which he is aware of being) it shall be given".***

Good, bad or indifferent, it does not matter, man receives multiplied a hundredfold that which he is aware of being.

In keeping with this changeless law,

> *"To him that hath not, it shall be taken from him and added to the one that hath",*

the rich get richer and the poor get poorer. You can only magnify that which you are conscious of being.

All things gravitate to that consciousness with which they are in tune.

Likewise, all things disentangle themselves from that consciousness with which they are out of tune.

~~~~~~~~~

> ***"I AM the Resurrection and the Life; he that believeth in Me, though he were dead, yet shall he live."***

The mystery of the crucifixion and the resurrection is so interwoven that, to be fully understood, the two must be explained together for one determines the other.

This mystery is symbolized on earth in the rituals of Good Friday and Easter. You have observed that the anniversary of this cosmic event, announced every year by the church, is not a fixed date as are other anniversaries marking births and deaths, but that this day changes from year to year, falling anywhere from the 22nd day of March to the 25th day of April.

The day of resurrection is determined in this manner.

The first Sunday after the full moon in Aries is celebrated as Easter. Aries begins on the 21st day of March and ends approximately on the 19th day of April. The sun's entry into Aries marks the beginning of Spring. The moon in its monthly transit around the earth will form sometime between March 21st and April 25th an opposition to the sun, which opposition is called a full moon.

The first Sunday after this phenomenon of the heavens occurs is celebrated as Easter; the Friday preceding this day is observed as Good Friday.

This movable date should tell the observant one to look for some interpretation other than the one commonly accepted. These days do not mark the anniversaries of the death and resurrection of an individual who lived on earth.

Seen from the earth, the sun in its northern passage appears at the Spring season of the year to cross the imaginary line man calls the equator.

So it is said by the mystic to be crossified or crucified, that man might live. It is significant that soon after this event takes place, all nature begins to arise or resurrect itself from its long Winter's sleep. Therefore, it may be concluded that this disturbance of nature, at this season of the year, is due directly to this crossing. Thus, it is believed that the sun must shed its blood on the Passover.

If these days marked the death and resurrection of a man, they would be fixed so that they would fall on the same date every year as all other historical events are fixed, but obviously this is not the case.

These dates were not intended to mark the anniversaries of the death and resurrection of Jesus, the man. The scriptures are psychological dramas and will reveal their meaning only as they are interpreted psychologically.

Neville Goddard's Interpretation of Scripture

These dates are adjusted to coincide with the cosmic change which occurs at this time of the year, marking the death of the old year and the beginning or resurrecting of the new year or Spring.

These dates do symbolize the death and resurrection of the Lord; but this Lord is not a man; it is your awareness of being. It is recorded that He gave His life that you might live,

> "I AM come that you might have life
> and that you might have it more abundantly."

Consciousness slays itself by detaching itself from that which it is conscious of being so that it may live to that which it desires to be.

Spring is the time of year when the millions of seeds, which all Winter lay buried in the ground, suddenly spring into visibility that man might live; and, because the mystical drama of the crucifixion and resurrection is in the nature of this yearly change, it is celebrated at this Spring season of the year; but, actually, it is taking place every moment of time.

The being who is crucified is your awareness of being. The cross is your conception of yourself. The resurrection is the lifting into visibility of this conception of yourself.

Far from being a day of mourning, Good Friday should be a day of rejoicing, for there can be no resurrection or expression unless there is first a crucifixion or impression.

The thing to be resurrected in your case is that which you desire to be. To do this, you must feel yourself to be the thing desired. You must feel

> "I AM the resurrection and the life of the desire".

I AM (your awareness of being) is the power resurrecting and making alive that which in your awareness you desire to be.

Neville Goddard's Interpretation of Scripture

~~~~~~~~~

"Two shall agree on touching anything and I shall establish it on earth"

The two agreeing are you (your awareness . . the consciousness desiring) and the thing desired.

When this agreement is attained, the crucifixion is completed; two have crossed or crossified each other.

<p align="center">I AM and THAT,</p>

consciousness and that which you are conscious of being, have joined and are one; I AM now nailed or fixed in the belief that I AM this fusion.

Jesus or I AM is nailed upon the cross of that. The nail that binds you upon the cross is the nail of feeling. The mystical union is now consummated and the result will be the birth of a child or the resurrection of a son bearing witness of his Father. Consciousness is united to that which it is conscious of being.

The world of expression is the child confirming this union. The day you cease to be conscious of being that which you are now conscious of being, that day your child or expression shall die and return to the bosom of his father, the faceless, formless awareness.

All expressions are the results of such mystical unions. So the priests are correct when they say that true marriages are made in heaven and can only be dissolved in heaven.

But let me clarify this statement by telling you that heaven is not a locality; it is a state of consciousness.

<p align="center">The Kingdom of Heaven is within you.</p>

In Heaven (consciousness) God is touched by that which he is aware of being.

> *"Who has touched me?*
> *For I perceive virtue has gone out of me"*

The moment this touching (feeling) takes place, there is an offspring or going-out-of-me into visibility taking place.

~~~~~~~~~

A person who directs a malicious thought to another will be injured by its rebound if he fails to get subconscious acceptance of the other.

> *"As ye sow, so shall ye reap."*

Furthermore, what you can wish and believe of another can be wished and believed of you, and you have no power to reject it if the one who desires it for you accepts it as true of you.

The only power to reject a subjective word is to be incapable of wishing a similar state of another . . to give, presupposes the ability to receive.

The possibility to impress an idea upon another mind presupposes the ability of that mind to receive that impression. Fools exploit the world; the wise transfigure it.

It is the highest wisdom to know that in the living universe there is no destiny other than that created out of imagination of man.

There is no influence outside of the mind of man.

> *"Whatsoever things are lovely, whatsoever are of good report;*
> *if there be any virtue and if there be any praise,*

> *think on these things."*

Never accept as true of others what you would not want to be true of you. To awaken a state within another it must first be awake within you. The state you would transmit to another can only be transmitted, if it is believed by you.

> Therefore to give is to receive.

You cannot give what you do not have and you have only what you believe.

So to believe a state as true of another not only awakens that state within the other but it makes it alive within you.

> You are what you believe.

> *"Give and ye shall receive, full measure, pressed down and running over."*

Giving is simply believing, for what you truly believe of others you will awaken within them.

~~~~~~~~~

According to the Scriptures, we sleep with Adam and wake with Christ. That is, we sleep collectively and wake individually.

> *"And the Lord God caused a deep sleep to fall upon Adam, and he slept."*

If Adam, or generic man, is in a deep sleep, then his experiences as recorded in the Scriptures must be a dream. Only he who is awake can tell his dream, and only he would understand the symbolism of dreams can interpret the dream.

> *"And they said one to another,*
> *Did not our heart burn within us,*
> *while He talked with us by the way,*
> *and while He opened to us the*
> *Scriptures?"*

The Bible is a revelation of the laws and functions of Mind expressed in the language of that twilight realm into which we go when we sleep.

Because the symbolical language of this twilight realm is much the same for all men, the recent explorers of this realm, human imagination, call it the "collective unconscious."

~~~~~~~~~

Take no thought of tomorrow; tomorrow's expressions are determined by today's impressions.

> *"Now is the accepted time."*
>
> *"The Kingdom of Heaven is at hand."*
>
> Jesus (salvation) said,
>
> *"I AM with you always."*

Your awareness is the savior that is with you always; but, if you deny Him, He will deny you also. You deny Him by claiming that He will appear, as millions today are claiming that salvation is to come; this is the equivalent of saying,

> "We are not saved".

You must stop looking for your savior to appear and begin claiming that you are already saved, and the signs of your claims will follow.

We are ever that which is defined by our awareness. Never claim,

"I shall be that".

Let all claims from now on be,

"I AM that I AM".

Before we ask, we are answered. The solution of any problem associated with desire is obvious. Every problem automatically produces the desire of solution.

Man is schooled in the belief that his desires are things against which he must struggle.

In his ignorance, he denies his savior who is constantly knocking at the door of consciousness to be let in (I AM the door). Would not your desire, if realized, save you from your problem? To let your savior in is the easiest thing in the world. Things must be, to be let in.

You are conscious of a desire; the desire is something you are aware of now. Your desire, though invisible, must be affirmed by you to be something that is real.

"God calleth those things which be not (are not seen) as though they were."

Claiming I AM the thing desired, I let the savior in.

"In whom also ye are circumcised with the circumcision made without hands; in putting off the body of the sins

of the flesh by circumcision of Christ."

Circumcision is the operation which removes the veil that hides the head of creation.

The physical act has nothing to do with the spiritual act.

The whole world could be physically circumcised and yet remain unclean and blind leaders of the blind. The spiritually circumcised have had the veil of darkness removed and know themselves to be Christ, the light of the world.

Let me now perform the spiritual operation on you, the reader.

This act is performed on the eighth day after birth, not because this day has any special significance or in any way differs from other days, but it is performed on this eighth day because eight is the figure which has neither beginning nor end.

Furthermore, the ancients symbolized the eighth numeral or letter as an enclosure or veil within and behind which lay buried the mystery of creation.

Thus, the secret of the operation on the eighth day is in keeping with the nature of the act, which act is to reveal the eternal head of creation, that changeless something in which all things begin and end and yet which remains its eternal self when all things cease to be.

This mysterious something is your awareness of being.

At this moment you are aware of being, but you are also aware of being someone. This someone is the veil that hides the being you really are.

You are first conscious of being, then you are conscious of being man. After the veil of man is placed upon your faceless self, you become conscious of being a member of a certain race, nation, family, creed etc.

The veil to be lifted, in spiritual circumcision, is the veil of man.

~~~~~~~~~

"He that is washed needeth not save to wash his feet, but is clean every whit."

Common sense would tell the reader that a man is not clean all over just, because his feet are washed.

Therefore, he should either discard this story as fantastic or else look for its hidden meaning. Every story of the Bible is a psychological drama taking place in the consciousness of man, and this one, is no exception.

This washing of the disciples' feet is the mystical story of spiritual circumcision or the revealing of the secrets of the Lord.

Jesus is called the Lord. You are told that the Lord's name is I AM . . Je Suis.

"I AM the Lord that is my name".

The story states that Jesus was naked save for a towel which covered his loins or secrets.

Jesus or Lord symbolizes your awareness of being whose secrets are hidden by the towel (consciousness of man).

The foot symbolizes the understanding which must be washed of all human beliefs or conceptions of itself by the Lord.

As the towel is removed to dry the feet, the secrets of the Lord are revealed.

In short, the removing of the belief that you are man reveals your awareness as the head of creation.

> Man is the foreskin hiding the head of creation.

> I AM the Lord hidden by the veil of man.

~~~~~~~~~

In the 26th verse of the first chapter of Genesis, it is stated,

"And God said, Let Us make man in Our image."

The churches refer to this plurality of Gods as God the Father, God the Son and God the Holy Spirit.

What is meant by "God the Father, God the Son and God the Holy Spirit" they have never attempted to explain, for they are in the dark concerning this mystery.

The Father, Son and Holy Spirit are three aspects or conditions of the unconditioned awareness of being called God.

The consciousness of being precedes the consciousness of being something. That unconditioned awareness which preceded all states of awareness is God . . I AM.

The three conditioned aspects or divisions of itself can best be told in this manner:

The receptive attitude of mind is that aspect which receives impressions and therefore may be likened to a womb or Mother.

That which makes the impression is the male or pressing aspect and is therefore known as Father.

The impression in time becomes an expression, which expression is ever the likeness and image of the impression; therefore this objectified aspect is said to be the Son bearing witness of his Father-Mother.

An understanding of this mystery of the trinity enables the one who understands it to completely transform his world and fashion it to his own liking.

~~~~~~~~

"I AM the beginning and the end"

reveals my consciousness as the cause of the birth and death of all expression.

"I AM hath sent me"

reveals my consciousness to be the Lord which sends me into the world in the image and likeness of that which I am conscious of being to live in a world composed of all that I am conscious of.

"I AM the Lord, and there is no God beside me,"

declares my consciousness to be the one and only Lord and beside my consciousness there is no God.

"Be still and know that I AM God"

means that I should still the mind and know that consciousness is God.

"Thou shalt not take the Name of the Lord thy God in vain."

"I AM the Lord: that is My Name."

Now that you have discovered your I AM, your consciousness to be God, do not claim anything to be true of yourself that you would not claim to be true of God, for in defining yourself, you are defining God.

That which you are conscious of being is that which you have named God. God and man are one. You and your Father are one.

Your unconditioned consciousness, or I AM, and that which you are conscious of being, are one. The conceiver and the conception are one.

If your conception of yourself is less than that which you claim as true of God, you have robbed God, the Father, because you (the Son or conception) bear witness of the Father or conceiver.

Do not take the magical Name of God, I AM, in vain for you will not be held guiltless; you must express all that you claim yourself to be. Name God by consciously defining yourself as your highest ideal.

~~~~~~~~~

The wise and disciplined man sees no barrier to the realization of his desire; he sees nothing to destroy. With a fixed attitude of mind he recognizes that the thing desired is already fully expressed, for he knows that a fixed subjective state, has ways and means of expressing itself, of which no man knows.

"Before they ask I have answered."

"I have ways ye know not of."

"My ways are past finding out."

The undisciplined man, on the other hand, constantly sees opposition to the fulfillment of his desire, and, because of the frustration, he forms desires of destruction which he firmly believes must be expressed before his basic desire can be realized.

When man discovers this law of one consciousness he will understand the great wisdom of the Golden Rule and so he will live by it and prove to himself that the kingdom of heaven is on earth.

You will realize why you should "do unto others that which you would have them do unto you." You will know why you should live by this Golden Rule because you will discover that it is just good common sense to do so since the rule is based upon life's changeless law and is no respecter of persons.

Consciousness is the one and only reality.

~~~~~~~~~

"And Jesus said unto them, Because of your unbelief; for verily I say unto you, if ye have faith as a grain of mustard seed, ye shall say unto this mountain, remove hence to yonder place; and it shall remove; and nothing shall be impossible unto you."

This faith of a grain of mustard seed has proved a stumbling block to man. He has been taught to believe that a grain of mustard seed signifies a small degree of faith. So he naturally wonders why he, a mature man, should lack this insignificant measure of faith when so small an amount assures success.

"Faith," he is told, *"is the substance of things hoped for, the evidence of things not seen."*

And again,

"Through faith... the worlds were framed by the word of God, so that things which are seen were not made of things which do appear."

Invisible things were made visible. The grain of mustard seed is not the measure of a small amount of faith. On the contrary, it is the absolute in faith. A mustard seed is conscious of being a mustard seed and a mustard seed alone. It is not aware of any other seed in the world. It is sealed in the conviction that it is a mustard seed in the same manner that the spermatozoa sealed in the womb is conscious of being man and only man.

A grain of mustard seed is truly the measure of faith necessary to accomplish your every objective; but like the mustard seed you too must lose yourself in the consciousness of being only the thing desired.

You abide within this sealed state until it bursts itself and reveals your conscious claim.

Faith is feeling or living in the consciousness of being the thing desired; faith is the secret of creation, the VAU in the divine name JOD HE VAU HE; faith is the Ham in the family of Noah; faith is the sense of feeling by which Isaac blessed and made real his son Jacob.

By faith, God (your consciousness), calleth things that are not seen as though they were and makes them seen.

It is faith which enables you to become conscious of being the thing desired; again, it is faith which seals you in this conscious state until your invisible claim ripens to maturity and expresses itself, is made visible. Faith or feeling is the secret of this appropriation. Through feeling, the consciousness desiring is joined to the thing desired.

How would you feel if you were that which you desire to be?

Wear the mood, this feeling that would be yours if you were already that which you desire to be; and in a little while you will be sealed in the belief that you are. Then without effort this invisible state will objectify itself; the invisible will be made visible.

If you had the faith of a grain of mustard seed, you would this day, through the magical substance of feeling, seal yourself in the consciousness of being that which you desire to be. In this mental stillness or tomblike state you would remain, confident that you need no one to roll away the stone, for all the mountains, stones and inhabitants of earth are nothing in your sight.

~~~~~~~~~

"I AM the Lord… there is no God beside Me;"

"The Word was made flesh and dwelt among us;"

and

"He sent His word and healed him."

You too can send your word, God's Word, and heal a friend. Is there something that you would like to hear of a friend? Define this something that you know he would love to be or to possess. Now with your desire properly defined you have a Word of God.

To send this Word on its way, to speak this Word into being, you simply do this.

Sit quietly where you are and assume the mental attitude of listening; recall your friend's voice; with this familiar voice established in your consciousness, imagine that you are actually hearing his voice and that he is telling you that he is or has that which you wanted him to be or to have. Impress upon your consciousness the fact that you actually heard him and that he told you what you wanted to hear; feel the thrill of having heard. Then drop it completely.

This is the mystic's secret of sending words into expression, of making the word flesh.

You form within yourself the word, the thing you want to hear; then you listen, and tell it to yourself.

"Speak, Lord, for thy servant heareth."

Your consciousness is the Lord speaking through the familiar voice of a friend and impressing on yourself that which you desire to hear. This self-impregnation, the state impressed upon yourself, the Word, has ways and means of expressing itself of which no man knows.

As you succeed in making the impression you will be unmoved by appearances for this self-impression is sealed as a grain of mustard seed and will in due season mature to its full expression.

~~~~~~~~

Prayer is an art and requires practice. The first requirement is a controlled imagination. Parade and vain repetitions are foreign to prayer. Its exercise requires tranquility and peace of mind,

"Use not vain repetitions,"

for prayer is done in secret

and

> *"thy Father which seeth in secret
> shall reward thee openly."*

The ceremonies that are customarily used in prayer are mere superstitions and have been invented to give prayer an air of solemnity. Those who do practice the art of prayer are often ignorant of the laws that control it. They attribute the results obtained to the ceremonies and mistake the letter for the spirit.

The essence of prayer is faith; but faith must be permeated with understanding to be given that active quality which it does not possess when standing alone.

> *"Therefore, get wisdom; and with all
> thy getting get understanding."*

~~~~~~~~~

"I and my Father are one but my Father is greater than I."

The conscious and subconscious are one, but the subconscious is greater than the conscious.

> *"I of myself can do nothing, the Father within
> me He doeth the work."*

I, objective consciousness, of myself can do nothing; the Father, the subconscious, He doeth the work. The subconscious is that in which everything is known, in which everything is possible, to which everything goes, from which everything comes, which belongs to all, to which all have access.

What we are conscious of is constructed out of what we are not conscious of. Not only do our subconscious assumptions influence our behavior but they also fashion the pattern of our objective existence. They alone have the power to say,

> "Let us make man . . objective manifestations . . in our image, after our likeness."

The whole of creation is asleep within the deep of man and is awakened to objective existence by his subconscious assumptions.

~~~~~~~~~

"Except your righteousness shall exceed the righteousness of the scribes and Pharisees, ye shall in no wise enter into the Kingdom of Heaven."

Scribes and Pharisees means those who are influenced and governed by the outer appearances, the rules and customs of the society in which they live, the vain desire to be thought well of, by other men.

Unless this state of mind is exceeded, your life will be one of limitation, of failure to attain your desires, of missing the mark . . of sin.

This righteousness is exceeded by true righteousness, which is always the consciousness of already being that which you want to be.

One of the greatest pitfalls in attempting to use the law of assumption is focusing your attention on things, on a new home, a better job, a bigger bank balance.

This is not the righteousness without which you

> "die in your sins."

Righteousness is not the thing itself; it is the consciousness, the feeling of already being the person you want to be, of already having the thing you desire.

> *"Seek ye first the Kingdom of God and His righteousness; and all these things shall be added unto you."*

The kingdom (entire creation) of God (your I AM) is within you.

Righteousness is the awareness that you already possess it all.

~~~~~~~~~

Prayer is the key which unlocks the infinite storehouse.

"Prove me now herewith, saith the Lord of hosts, if I will not open you the windows of heaven, and pour you out a blessing, that there shall not be room enough to receive it."

Prayer modifies or completely changes our subconscious assumptions, and a change of assumption is a change of expression.

The conscious mind reasons inductively from observation, experience and education. It therefore finds it difficult to believe what the five senses and inductive reason deny.

The subconscious reasons deductively and is never concerned with the truth or falsity of the premise, but proceeds on the assumption of the correctness of the premise and objectifies results which are consistent with the premise.

This distinction must be clearly seen by all who would master the art of praying.

No true grasp of the science of prayer can be really obtained until the laws governing the dual nature of consciousness are understood and the importance of the subconscious realized.

Prayer . . the art of believing what is denied by the senses . . deals almost entirely with the subconscious. Through prayer, the subconscious is suggested, into acceptance of the wish fulfilled, and, reasoning deductively, logically unfolds it to its legitimate end.

"Far greater is He that is in you than he that is in the world."

~~~~~~~~~

"Thou shalt decree a thing and it shall be established unto thee."

It is not a strong will that sends the subjective word on its mission, so much as it is clear thinking and feeling, the truth of the state affirmed. When belief and will are in conflict, belief invariably wins.

"Not by might, nor by power, but by my spirit, saith the Lord of hosts."

It is not what you want that you attract; you attract what you believe to be true.

Therefore, get into the spirit of these mental conversations and give them the same degree of reality that you would a telephone conversation.

"If thou canst believe, all things are possible to him that believeth. Therefore, I say unto you, what things soever you desire, when you pray, believe that ye received them, and ye shall have them."

The acceptance of the end wills the means. And the wisest reflection could not devise more effective means than those which are willed by the acceptance of the end. Mentally talk to your friends as though your desires for them were already realized.

Imagination is the beginning of the growth of all forms, and faith is the substance out of which they are formed.

By imagination, that which exists in latency or is asleep within the deep of consciousness is awakened and is given form.

The cures attributed to the influence of certain medicines, relics and places are the effects of imagination and faith. The curative power is not in the spirit that is in them, it is in the spirit in which they are accepted.

~~~~~~~~~

> **"I AM is that which,
> amid unnumbered forms,
> is ever the same."**

This great discovery of cause reveals that, good or bad, man is actually the arbiter of his own fate, and that it is his concept of himself that determines the world in which he lives [and his concept of himself is his reactions to life].

In other words, if you are experiencing ill health, knowing the truth about cause, you cannot attribute the illness to anything other than to the particular arrangement of the basic cause-substance, an arrangement which [was produced by your reactions to life, and] is defined by your concept "I am unwell". This is why you are told

> "Let the weak man say, 'I AM strong'",

for by his assumption, the cause-substance . . I AM . . is rearranged and must, therefore, manifest that which its rearrangement affirms. This principle governs every aspect of your life, be it social, financial, intellectual, or spiritual.

I AM is that reality to which, whatever happens, we must turn for an explanation of the phenomena of life. It is I AM's concept of itself that determines the form and scenery of its existence.

Everything depends upon its attitude towards itself; that which it will not affirm as true of itself cannot awaken in its world.

That is, your concept of yourself, such as

"I AM strong", "I AM secure", "I AM loved",

determines the world in which you live. In other words, when you say, "I am a man, I am a father, I am an American", you are not defining different I AM's; you are defining different concepts or arrangements of the one cause-substance, the one I AM. Even in the phenomena of nature, if the tree were articulate, it would say, "I am a tree, an apple tree, a fruitful tree".

When you know that consciousness is the one and only reality, conceiving itself to be something good, bad or indifferent, and becoming that which it conceived itself to be, you are free from the tyranny of second causes, free from the belief that there are causes outside of your own mind that can affect your life.

In the state of consciousness of the individual is found the explanation of the phenomena of life. If man's concept of himself were different, everything in his world would be different.

His concept of himself being what it is, everything in his world must be as it is.

Thus it is abundantly clear that there is only one I AM and you are that I AM.

And while I AM is infinite, you, by your concept of yourself, are displaying only a limited aspect of the infinite I AM.

~~~~~~~~~

An assumption builds a bridge of incidents that lead inevitably to the fulfillment of itself.

Man believes the future to be the natural development of the past. But the law of assumption clearly shows that this is not the case. Your assumption places you psychologically where you are not physically; then your senses pull you back from where you were psychologically to where you are physically. It is these psychological forward motions that produce your physical forward motions in time. Precognition permeates all the scriptures of the world.

> *"In my Father's house are many mansions;*
> *If it were not so, I would have told you. I*
> *go to prepare a place for you. And if I go*
> *and prepare a place for you, I will come*
> *again and receive you unto myself:*
> *that where I am, there ye may be also...*
> *And now I have told you before it came*
> *to pass, that, when it is come to pass,*
> *ye might believe."*

The "I" in this quotation is your imagination, which goes into the future, into one of the many mansions. Mansion is the state desired... telling of an event before it occurs physically is simply feeling yourself into the state desired until it has the tone of reality. You go and prepare a place for yourself by imagining yourself into the feeling of your wish fulfilled.

Then, you speed from this state of the wish fulfilled, where you have not been physically, back to where you were physically a moment ago. Then, with an irresistible forward movement, you move forward across a series of events to the physical realization of your wish, that where you have been in imagination, there you will be in the flesh also.

~~~~~~~~~

"Not My Will, but Thine be done."

"I will be" is a confession that "I am not". The Father's Will is always "I AM".

Until you realize that you are the Father (there is only one I AM, and your infinite self is that I AM), your will is always "I will be".

In the law of assumption, your consciousness of being is the Father's will. The mere wish without this consciousness is the "my will".

This great quotation, so little understood, is a perfect statement of the law of assumption.

It is impossible to do anything. You must be in order to do.

If you had a different concept of yourself, everything would be different. You are what you are, so everything is as it is. The events which you observe are determined by the concept you have of yourself. If you change your concept of yourself, the events ahead of you in time are altered, but, thus altered, they form again a deterministic sequence starting from the moment of this changed concept.

You are a being with powers of intervention, which enable you, by a change of consciousness, to alter the course of observed events, in fact, to change your future.

Deny the evidence of the senses, and assume the feeling of the wish fulfilled.

Inasmuch as your assumption is creative and forms an atmosphere, your assumption, if it be a noble one, increases your assurance and helps you to reach a higher level of being.

If, on the other hand, your assumption be an unlovely one, it hinders you and makes your downward way swifter. Just as the lovely assumptions create a harmonious atmosphere, so the hard and bitter feelings create a hard and bitter atmosphere.

~~~~~~~~~

"He was in the world, and the world was made by Him and the world knew Him not. The mystery hid from the ages; Christ in you, the hope of glory."

The "He" in the first of these quotations is your imagination.

As previously explained, there is only one substance. This substance is consciousness.

It is your imagination which forms this substance into concepts, which concepts are then manifested as conditions, circumstances, and physical objects.

Thus imagination made your world.

This supreme truth, with but few exceptions, man is not conscious of.

The mystery,

"Christ in you",

referred to in the second quotation, is your imagination, by which your world is molded.

The hope of glory is your awareness of the ability to rise perpetually to higher levels.

Christ is not to be found in history, nor in external forms.

You find Christ only when you become aware of the fact that your imagination is the only redemptive power.

When this is discovered, the "towers of dogma will have heard the trumpets of Truth, and, like the walls of Jericho, crumble to dust".

~~~~~~~~~

Man in the moment of his awakening to the imaginative life must meet the test of Sonship.

"Father, reveal Thy Son in me"

And

"It pleased God to reveal His Son in me".

The supreme test of Sonship is the forgiveness of sin. The test that your imagination is Christ Jesus, the Son of God, is your ability to forgive sin.

Sin means missing one's mark in life, falling short of one's ideal, failing to achieve one's aim.

Forgiveness means identification of man with his ideal or aim in life.

This is the work of awakened imagination, the supreme work, for it tests man's ability to enter into and partake of the nature of his opposite.

> *"Let the weak man say, I AM strong."*

Reasonably, this is impossible. Only awakened imagination can enter into and partake of the nature of its opposite.

~~~~~~~~~

> **"All things when they are admitted are made manifest by the light: for everything that is made manifest is light,"**

and

> **"Ye are the light of the world,"**

by which those ideas to which you have consented are made manifest.

Hold fast to your ideal. Nothing can take it from you but your imagination. Don't think of your ideal, think from it. It is only the ideals from which you think that are ever realized.

> *"Man lives not by bread alone, but by every word that proceeds out of the mouth of God"*

and

> *"the mouth of God"* is the mind of man.

Become a drinker and an eater of the ideals you wish to realize.

Have a set, definite aim or your mind will wander, and wandering it eats every negative suggestion. If you live right mentally, everything else will be right. By a change of mental diet, you can alter the course of observed events. But unless there is a change of mental diet, your personal history remains the same.

You illuminate or darken your life by the ideas to which you consent. Nothing is more important to you than the ideas on which you feed. And you feed on the ideas from which you think. If you find the world unchanged, it is a sure sign that you are wanting in fidelity to the new mental diet, which you neglect in order to condemn your environment. You are in need of a new and sustained attitude.

You can be anything you please if you will make the conception habitual, for any idea which excludes all others from the field of attention discharges in action.

The ideas and moods to which you constantly return define the state with which you are fused. Therefore train yourself to occupy more frequently the feeling of your wish fulfilled. This is creative magic. It is the way to work toward fusion with the desired state.

If you would assume the feeling of your wish fulfilled more frequently, you would be master of your fate, but unfortunately you shut out your assumption for all but the occasional hour. Practice making real to yourself the feeling of the wish fulfilled.

After you have assumed the feeling of the wish fulfilled, do not close the experience as you would a book, but carry it around like a fragrant odor.

Instead of being completely forgotten, let it remain in the atmosphere communicating its influence automatically to your actions and reactions. A mood, often repeated, gains a momentum that is hard to break or check. So be careful of the feelings you entertain. Habitual moods reveal the state with which you are fused.

It is always possible to pass from thinking of the end you desire to realize, to thinking from the end.

But the crucial matter is thinking from the end, for thinking from means unification or fusion with the idea: whereas in thinking of the end, there is always subject and object . . the thinking individual and the thing thought.

You must imagine yourself into the state of your wish fulfilled, in your love for that state, and in so doing, live and think from it and no more of it. You pass from thinking of to thinking from by centering your imagination in the feeling of the wish fulfilled.

~~~~~~~~~

"And, behold, the Lord stood above it."
The Lord and meaning are one . . the Creator,
the cause of the phenomena of life.
"In the beginning was the Word, and
the Word was with God, and the Word
was God."

In the beginning was the intention, the meaning, and the intention was with the intender, and the intention was the intender.

The objects and events in time and space occupy a lower level of significance than the level of meaning which produced them.

All things were made by meaning, and without meaning was not anything made that was made. The fact that everything seen can be regarded as the effect, on a lower level of significance, of an unseen higher order of significance is a very important one to grasp.

Our usual mode of procedure is to attempt to explain the higher levels of significance, why things happen, in terms of the lower, what and how things happen.

For example, let us take an actual accident and try to explain it.

Most of us live on the level of what happened . . the accident was an event in space . . one automobile struck another and practically demolished it.

Some of us live on the higher level of "how" the accident happened . . it was a rainy night, the roads were slippery and the second car skidded into the first.

On rare occasions, a few of us reach the highest or causal level of "why" such an accident occurs. Then we become aware of the invisible, the state of consciousness which produced the visible event.

In this case, the ruined car was driven by a widow, who, though she felt she could not afford to, greatly desired to change her environment. Having heard that, by the proper use of her imagination, she could do and be all she wished to be, this widow had been imagining herself actually living in the city of her desire.

At the same time, she was living in a consciousness of loss, both personal and financial. Therefore, she brought upon herself an event which was seemingly another loss, but the sum of money the insurance company paid her allowed her to make the desired change in her life.

When we see the "why" behind the seeming accident, the state of consciousness that produced the accident, we are led to the conclusion that there is no accident. Everything in life has its invisible meaning.

The man who learns of an accident, the man who knows "how" it happened, and the man who knows "why" it happened are on three different levels of awareness in regard to that accident.

On the ascending scale, each higher level carries us a step in advance towards the truth of the accident.

We should strive constantly to lift ourselves to the higher level of meaning, the meaning that is always invisible and above the physical event. But, remember, the meaning or cause of the phenomena of life can be found only within the consciousness of man.

Man is so engrossed in the visible side of the drama of life . . the side of "what" has happened, and "how" it happened . . that he rarely rises to the invisible side of "why" it happened. He refuses to accept the Prophet's warning that:

> *"Things which are seen*
> *were not made of things*
> *that do appear."*

His descriptions of "what" has happened and "how" it happened are true in terms of his corresponding level of thought, but when he asks "why" it happened, all physical explanations break down and he is forced to seek the "why", or meaning of it, on the invisible and higher level.

The mechanical analysis of events deals only with external relationships of things. Such a course will never reach the level which holds the secret of why the events happen. Man must recognize that the lower and visible sides flow from the invisible and higher level of meaning.

Intuition is needed to lift us up to the level of meaning, to the level of why things happen.

Let us follow the advice of the Hebrew prophet of old and

"lift up our eyes unto the hills"

within ourselves, and observe what is taking place there. See what ideas we have accepted as true, what states we have consented to, what dreams, what desires, and, above all, what intentions.

It is from these hills that all things come to reveal our stature, our height, on the vertical scale of meaning.

If we lift our eyes to

"the Thee in Me who works behind the Veil",

we will see the meaning of the phenomena of life.

~~~~~~~~~

The Bible uses many images to symbolize Truth, but the images used symbolize Truth on different levels of meaning. On the lowest level, the image used is stone. For example:

> *"... a great stone was upon The well's mouth. And thither were all the flocks gathered: and they rolled the stone from the well's mouth, and watered the sheep..."*

> *"...They sank into the bottom as a stone."*

When a stone blocks the well, it means that people have taken these great symbolical revelations of truth literally. When someone rolls the stone away, it means that an individual has discovered beneath the allegory or parable its psychological life germ, or meaning.

This hidden meaning which lies behind the literal words is symbolized by water. It is this water. In the form of psychological Truth, that he then offers to humanity.

"The flock of my pasture are men."

The literal-minded man who refuses the

"cup of water"

psychological Truth offered him,

"sinks into the bottom as a stone."

He remains on the level where he sees everything in pure objectivity, without any subjective relationship he may keep all the commandments . . written on stone . . literally, and yet break them psychologically all day long.

He may, for example not literally steal the property of another, and yet see the other in want. To see another in want, is to rob him of his birthright as a child of God.

For we are all "children of the most high."

*"And if children, then heirs;
heirs of God, and joint-heirs
with Christ..."*

To know what to do about a seeming misfortune is to have the

"cup of water"

the psychological truth, that could save the situation. But such knowledge is not enough.

Man must not only

"fill the water pots of stone with water"

that is, discover the psychological truth

"into wine."

This he does by living a life according to the truth which he has discovered.

Only by such use of the truth can he

"taste the water that was made wine..."

A mans birthright is to be Jesus. He is born to

"save his people from their sins"

... But the salvation of a man is

"not by water only, but by water and blood".

To know what to do to save yourself or another is not enough; you must do it.

Knowledge of what to do is water; doing it is blood.

This is he that came

"not by water only, but by water and blood."

The whole of this mystery is in the conscious, active use of imagination to appropriate that particular state of consciousness that would save you or another from the present limitation. Outward ceremonies cannot accomplish this.

~~~~~~~~

God is your consciousness.

His promises are conditional. Unless the demand, your state of consciousness, is changed, the supply . . the present conditions of your life, remain as they are.

"As we forgive"

as we change our mind, the law is automatic. Your state of consciousness is the spring of action, the directing force, and that which creates the supply.

*"If that nation, against whom
I have pronounced, turn from
their evil, I will repent of the
evil that I thought to do unto them.
And at what instant I shall speak
concerning a nation, and concerning
a kingdom, to build and to
plant it;*

*If it do evil in my sight, that it
obey not my voice, then I will
repent of the good, wherewith I
said I would benefit them."*

This statement of Jeremiah suggests that a commitment is involved if the individual or nation would realize the goal, a commitment to certain fixed attitudes of mind.

The feeling of the wish fulfilled is a necessary condition in mans search for the goal.

The story I am about to tell you shows that man is what the observer has the capacity to see in him; that what he is seen to be is a direct index to the observer's state of consciousness. This story is, also, a challenge to us all to

"shed our blood",

use our imagination lovingly on behalf of another.

There is no day that passes that does not afford us the opportunity to transform a life by the shedding of our blood.

"Without the shedding of blood there is no remission."

One night in New York City I was able to unveil the mystery of the

"water and the blood"

to a school teacher. I had quoted the above statement from Hebrews 9:22, and went on to explain that the realization that we have no hope save in ourselves is the discovery that God is within us . . that this discovery causes the dark caverns of the skull to grow luminous, and we know that:

"The spirit of man is the candle of the lord"...

and that this realization is the light to guide us safely over the earth.

*"His Candle shined upon my
head and by his light I walked
through darkness"*

However, we must not look upon this radiant light of the head as God, for man is the image of God.

"God appears, and God is light,
To those poor souls who dwell in Night;
But does a Human Form display
To those who dwell in realms of
Day."
. . . Blake

But this must be experienced to be known. There is no other way, and no other man's experience can be a substitute for our own.

I told the teacher that her change of attitude in regard to another would produce a corresponding change in the other; that such knowledge was the true meaning of the water mentioned in I. John 5:6, but that such knowledge alone was not enough to produce the rebirth desired; that such rebirth could only come to pass by

"water and blood",

or the application of this truth. Knowledge of what to do is the water of life, but doing it is the blood of the savior. In other words, a little knowledge, if carried out in action is more profitable than much knowledge which we neglect to carry out in action.

As I talked, one student kept impinging upon the teachers mind. But this, thought she, would be a too difficult case on which to test the truth of what I was telling her concerning the mystery of re-birth. All knew, teachers and students alike, that this particular student was incorrigible.

The outer facts of her case were these:

The teachers, including the principal and school psychiatrist, had sat in judgment on the student just a few days before. They had come to a unanimous decision that the girl, for the good of the school, must be expelled upon reaching her sixteenth birthday. She was rude, crude, unethical and used most vile language. The date for dismissal was but a month away.

As she rode home that night, the teacher kept wondering if she could really change her mind about the girls, and if so, would the student undergo a change of behavior because she herself had undergone a change of attitude?

The only way to find out would be to try.

This would be quite an undertaking for it meant assuming full responsibility for the incarnation of the new values in the student. Did she dare to assume so great a power, such creative, God-like power?

This meant a complete reversal of man's normal attitude towards life from

> "*I will love him if he first loves me*",

> to

> "*He loves me, because I first loved him.*"

> This was too much like playing God.

> "*We love him, because he first Loved us.*"

`But no matter how she tried to argue against it, the feeling persisted that my interpretation gave meaning to the mystery of re-birth by "water and blood."

The teacher decided to accept the challenge. And this is what she did.

`She brought the child's face before her mind's eye and saw her smile. She listened and imagined she heard the girl say "Good morning". This was something the student had never done since coming to that school. The teacher imagined the very best about the girl, and then listened and looked as though she heard and saw all that she would hear and see after these things should be. The teacher did this over and over again until she persuaded herself it was true, and fell asleep.

`The very next morning, the student entered her classroom and smilingly said "Good morning". The teacher was so surprised she almost did not respond, and, by her own confession, all through the day she looked for signs of the girl's returning to her former behavior.

'However, the girl continued in the transformed state. By the end of the week, the change was noted by all; a second staff meeting was called and a decision of expulsion was revoked. As the child remained friendly and gracious, the teacher has had to ask herself,

> "Where was the bad child in the first place?"
> "For Mercy, Pity, Peace, and Love
> Is God, Our father dear,
> And Mercy, Pity, Peace and Love
> Is man, His child and care." . . . Blake

Transformation is in principle always possible, for the transformed being lives in us, and it is only a question of becoming conscious of it.

The teacher had to experience this transformation to know the mystery of

> *"blood and water";*

there was no other way, and no mans experience could have been a substitute for her own.

> *"We have redemption through his blood."*

Without the decision to change her mind in regard to the child, and the imaginative power to carry it out, the teacher could never have redeemed the student.

None can know the redemptive power of the imagination who has not

> "shed his blood",

and tasted the cup of experience.

> "Once read thy own breast right,
> And thou hast done with fears!
> Man gets no other light,

Search he a thousand years."

.. Matthew Arnold

My body carries out the instructions given to it by my mind.

~~~~~~~~~

The drama of life is a psychological one which we bring to pass by our attitudes rather than by our acts. There is no escape from our present predicament except by a radical psychological transformation. Everything depends upon our attitude towards ourselves.

That which we will not affirm as true of ourselves will not develop in our lives.

We hear much of the humble man, the meek man, but what is meant by a meek man? He is not poor and groveling, the proverbial doormat, as he is generally conceived to be.

Men who make themselves as worms in their own sight have lost the vision of that life . . into the likeness of which it is the true purpose of the spirit to transform this life.

Men should take their measurements not from life as they see it but from men like Dr. Millikan, who, while poor and unproven, dared to assume, "I have a lavish, steady, dependable income, consistent with integrity and mutual benefit."

Such men are the meek of the Gospels, the men who inherit the earth.

Any concept of self less than the best, robs us of the earth.

The promise is,

"Blessed are the meek, for they shall inherit the earth."

In the original text, the word translated as meek is the opposite of the words, resentful, angry.

It has the meaning of becoming "tamed" as a wild animal is tamed. After the mind is tamed, it may be likened to a vine, of which it may be said,

"Behold this vine. I found it a wild tree whose wanton strength had swollen into irregular twigs. But I pruned the plant, and it grew temperate in its vain expense of useless leaves, and knotted as you see into these clean, full clusters to repay the hand that wisely wounded it."

A meek man is a self-disciplined man. He is so disciplined he sees only the finest, he thinks only the best. He is the one who fulfills the suggestion,

"Brethren, whatsoever things are true, whatsoever things are honest, whatsoever things are just, whatsoever things are pure, whatsoever things are lovely, whatsoever things are of good report; if there be any virtue and if there be any praise, think on these things."

We rise to a higher level of consciousness, not because we have curbed our passions, but because we have cultivated our virtues. In truth, a meek man is a man in complete control of his moods, and his moods are the highest, for he knows he must keep a high mood if he would walk with the highest.

It is my belief that all men can, like Dr. Millikan, change the course of their lives. I believe that Dr. Millikan's technique of making his desire a present fact to himself is of great importance to any seeker after the "truth."

It is also his high purpose to be of "mutual benefit" that is inevitably the goal of us all. It is much easier to imagine the good of all than to be purely selfish in our imagining.

By our imagination, by our affirmations, we can change our world, we can change our future. To the man of high purpose, to the disciplined man, this is a natural measure, so let us all become disciplined men.

~~~~~~~~~

We are creatures of habit; and habit, though not law, acts like the most compelling law in the world. With this knowledge of the power of imagination, be as the disciplined man and transform your world by imagining and feeling only what is lovely and of good report.

The beautiful idea you awaken in yourself shall not fail to arouse its affinity in others. Do not wait four months for the harvest. Today is the day to practice the control and discipline of your imagination.

Man is only limited by weakness of attention and poverty of imagination.

The great secret is a controlled imagination and a well sustained attention, firmly and repeatedly focused on the object to be accomplished.

> *"Now is the acceptable time to give beauty for ashes, joy for mourning, praise for the spirit of heaviness; that they might be called trees of righteousness, the planting of the Lord that He might be glorified."*

Now is the time to control our imagination and attention. By control, I do not mean restraint by will power but rather cultivation through love and compassion.

With so much of the world in discord we cannot possibly emphasize too strongly the power of imaginative love.

~~~~~~~~

Have you ever had a prayer answered?

What wouldn't men give just to feel certain that when they pray, something definite would happen. For this reason, I would like to take a little time to see why it is that some prayers are answered and some apparently fall on dry ground.

"When ye pray, believe that ye receive, and ye shall receive."

Believe that ye receive . . is the condition imposed upon man.

Unless we believe that we receive, our prayer will not be answered. A prayer granted implies that something is done in consequence of the prayer which otherwise would not have been done. Therefore, the one who prays is the spring of action, the directing mind, and the one who grants the prayer.

Such responsibility man refuses to assume, for responsibility it seems, is mankind's invisible nightmare.

The whole natural world is built on law. Yet, between prayer and its answer, we see no such relation. We feel that God may answer or ignore our prayer, that our prayer may hit the mark or may miss it.

The mind is still unwilling to admit that God subjects Himself to His own laws. How many people believe that there is, between prayer and its answer, a relation of cause and effect?

Let us take a look at the means employed to heal the ten lepers as related in the seventeenth chapter of the Gospel of St. Luke.

The thing that strikes us in this story is the method that was used to raise their faith to the needful intensity.

We are told that the ten lepers appealed to Jesus to "have mercy" on them, that is, to heal them.

Jesus ordered them to go and show themselves to the priests,

and

"As they went, they were cleansed."

The Mosaic Law demanded that when a leper recovered from his disease he must show himself to the priest to obtain a certificate of restored health. Jesus imposed a test upon the lepers' faith and supplied a means by which their faith could be raised to its full potency.

If the lepers refused to go . . they had no faith . . and, therefore, could not be healed. But, if they obeyed Him, the full realization of what their journey implied would break upon their minds as they went and this dynamic thought would heal them.

So, we read,

"As they went, they were cleansed."

You, no doubt, often have heard the words of that inspiring old hymn;

"Oh, what peace we often forfeit; oh, what needless pain we bear, all because we do not carry everything to God in prayer."

I, myself, came to this conviction through experience, being led to brood upon the nature of prayer. I believe in the practice and philosophy of what men call prayer, but not everything that receives that name is really prayer.

Prayer is the elevation of the mind to that which we seek.

~~~~~~~~~

The necessity of persistence in prayer is shown us in the Bible.

"Which of you,"

asked Jesus,

"shall go unto him at midnight, and say unto him: Friend, lend me three loaves; for a friend of mine is come to me from a journey, and I have nothing to set before him":

and he from within shall answer and say,

'Trouble me not; the door is now shut and my children are with me in bed; I cannot rise and give thee.' I say unto you, though he will not rise and give him because he is his friend, yet because of his importunity he will arise and give as many as he needeth."

The word translated as "importunity" means, literally, shameless impudence. We must persist until we succeed in imagining ourselves into the situation of the answered prayer.

The secret of success is found in the word "perseverance." The soul imagining itself into the act, takes on the results of the act. Not imagining itself into the act, it is ever free from the result.

Experience in imagination, what you would experience in reality were you already what you want to be, and you will take on the result of that act. Do not experience in imagination what you want to experience in reality and you will ever be free of the result.

"When ye pray, believe that ye receive, and ye shall receive."

One must persist until he reaches his friend on a higher level of consciousness. He must persist until his feeling of the wish fulfilled has all the sensory vividness of reality.

Prayer is a controlled waking dream. If we are to pray successfully, we must steady our attention to observe the world as it would be seen by us were our prayer answered.

Steadying attention makes no call upon any special faculty, but it does demand control of imagination. We must extend our senses . . observe our changed relationship to our world and trust this observation. The new world is not there to grasp, but to sense, to touch.

The best way to observe it is to be intensely aware of it. In other words, we can, by listening as though we heard and by looking as though we saw, actually hear voices and see scenes from within ourselves that are otherwise not audible or visible.

With our attention focused on the state desired, the outer world crumbles and then the world, like music, by a new setting, turns all its discords into harmonies.

    Life is not a struggle but a surrender.

Our prayers are answered by the powers we invoke not by those we exert.

So long as the eyes take notice, the soul is blind . . for the world that moves us is the one we imagine, not the world round about us.

We must yield our whole being to the feeling of being the noble one we want to be. If anything is kept back, the prayer is vain. We often are deprived of our high goal by our effort to possess it.

We are called upon to act on the assumption that we already are the man we would be. If we do this without effort . . experiencing in imagination what we would experience in the flesh had we realized our goal, we shall find that we do, indeed, possess it.

> The healing touch is in our attitude.

We need change nothing but our attitude towards it. Assume a virtue if you have it not, assume the feeling of your wish fulfilled.

> *"Pray for my soul; more things are wrought by prayer than this world dreams of."*

~~~~~~~~~

The Word of God, that is, the psychological teaching in the Bible, is to make a man different, first in thought and then in being, so that he becomes a new man or is born again.

Whenever an entirely new attitude enters into a person's life, psychological rebirth to some extent has occurred. Man wants to be better, not different.

The Bible speaks, not of being better, but of another man, a man reborn.

Neville Goddard's Interpretation of Scripture

"Except a man be born again,
he cannot see the Kingdom of God...
Except a man be born of water and the spirit,
he cannot enter into the Kingdom of God.
Marvel not that I said unto thee,
ye must be born again."

The Ten Commandments were written on tablets of stone for those incapable of seeing any deeper meaning. Stone represents the most external and literal form of spiritual truth, and water refers to another way of understanding the same truth. Wine or spirit is the highest form of understanding it.

"Such as men themselves are, such will God appear to them to be,"

wrote John Smith, the Cambridge Platonist.

"The God of the moralist is before all things a great judge and schoolmaster; the God of Science is impersonal and inflexible Vital Law; the God of the savage is the kind of chief he would be himself if he had the opportunity."

No man's conduct will be higher than his conception of God, and his conception of God is determined by the kind of man he, himself, is.

"For such as men themselves are,
such will God appear to them to be,"

and what is true of man's concept of God is equally true of man's concept of God's Word, the Bible. It will be to him what he is to himself.

"God is God from the creation,
Truth alone is man's salvation;
But the God that now you worship
Soon shall be your God no more

For the soul in its unfolding
Evermore its thoughts remolding,
Learns more truly in its progress
How to love and to adore."

~~~~~~~~~

**"Let these sayings sink down into your ears;
For the Son of Man shall be delivered
into the hands of men."**

Be not as those who have eyes that see not and ears that hear not.

Let these revelations sink deep into your ears, for after the Son (idea) is conceived, man with his false values (reason) will attempt to explain the why and wherefore of the Son's expression, and in so doing, will rend him to pieces.

After men have agreed that a certain thing is humanly impossible and therefore cannot be done, let someone accomplish the impossible thing; the wise ones who said it could not be done will begin to tell you why and how it happened. After they are all through tearing the seamless robe (cause of manifestation) apart, they will be as far from the truth as they were when they proclaimed it impossible.

As long as man looks for the cause of expression in places other than the expresser, he looks in vain.

For thousands of years, man has been told,

"I AM the resurrection and the life."

"No manifestation cometh unto me save I draw it",

but man will not believe it. He prefers to believe in causes outside of himself.

The moment that which was not seen becomes seen, man is ready to explain the cause and purpose of its appearance. Thus, the Son of Man (idea desiring manifestation) is constantly being destroyed at the hands of (reasonable explanation or wisdom) man.

Now that your awareness is revealed to you as cause of all expression, do not return to the darkness of Egypt with its many gods. There is but one God. The one and only God is your awareness.

> *"And all the inhabitants of the earth are reputed as nothing. And He doeth according to His will in the army of Heaven, and among the inhabitants of the earth and none can stay His hand, or say unto him what doest Thou?"*

If the whole world should agree that a certain thing could not be expressed and yet you became aware of being that, which they had agreed could not be expressed, you would express it.

Your awareness never asks permission to express that which you are aware of being. It does so, naturally and without effort, in spite of the wisdom of man and all opposition.

> *"Salute no man by the way"*

This is not a command to be insolent or unfriendly, but a reminder not to recognize a superior, not to see in anyone a barrier to your expression. None can stay your hand or question your ability to express that which you are conscious of being. Do not judge after the appearances of a thing,

> *"for all are as nothing in the eyes of God."*

When the disciples through their judgment of appearances saw the insane child, they thought it a more difficult problem to solve than others they had seen; and so they failed to achieve a cure. In judging after appearances, they forgot that all things were possible to God.

Hypnotized as they were by the reality of appearances, they could not feel the naturalness of sanity.

The only way for you to avoid such failures is to constantly bear in mind that your awareness is the Almighty, the all-wise presence. Without help, this unknown presence within you effortlessly out pictures that which you are aware of being.

Be perfectly indifferent to the evidence of the senses, so that you may feel the naturalness of your desire, and your desire will be realized. Turn from appearances and feel the naturalness of that perfect perception within yourself, a quality never to be distrusted or doubted. Its understanding will never lead you astray. Your desire is the solution of your problem. As the desire is realized, the problem is dissolved.

You cannot force anything outwardly by the mightiest effort of the will. There is only one way you can command the things you want and that is by assuming the consciousness of the things desired.

There is a vast difference between feeling a thing and merely knowing it intellectually.

You must accept without reservation the fact that by possessing (feeling) a thing in consciousness, you have commanded the reality that causes it to come into existence in concrete form.

You must be absolutely convinced of an unbroken connection between the invisible reality and its visible manifestation.

Your inner acceptance must become an intense, unalterable conviction which transcends both reason and intellect, renouncing entirely any belief in the reality of the externalization except as a reflection of an inner state of consciousness.

When you really understand and believe these things, you will have built up so profound a certainty that nothing can shake you.

Your desires are the invisible realities which respond only to the commands of God.

God commands the invisible to appear by claiming himself to be the thing commanded.

> *"He made Himself equal with God and found it not robbery to do the works of God."*

Now let this saying sink deep in your ear:

Be conscious of being, that which you want to appear.

Neville Goddard's Interpretation of Scripture

Metaphysical / Law of Attraction Books

David Allen - The Power of I AM (2014), The Power of I AM - Volume 2 (2015), The Power of I AM - Volume 3 (2017)

David Allen - The Creative Power of Thought, Man's Greatest Discovery (2017)

David Allen - The Secrets, Mysteries & Powers of The Subconscious Mind (2017)

David Allen - The Money Bible - The Secrets of Attracting Prosperity (2017)

David Allen - Your Faith Is Your Fortune, Your Unlimited Power (2018)

The Neville Goddard Collection (All 10 of his books plus 2 Lecture series) (2016)

Neville Goddard - Assumptions Harden Into Facts: The Book (2016)

Neville Goddard - Imagination: The Redemptive Power in Man (2016)

Neville Goddard - The World is At Your Command - The Very Best of Neville Goddard (2017)

Neville Goddard - Imagining Creates Reality - 365 Mystical Daily Quotes (2017)

Neville Goddard's Interpretation of Scripture (2018)

The Definitive Christian D. Larson Collection (6 Volumes, 30 books) (2014)

Visit us at **NevilleGoddardBooks.com** for 1000's of Free Downloadable eBooks on Metaphysics, Law of Attraction, Oriental Philosophy, Ancient Secrets, plus much more.

Also Check out our friends at **TheIAMLibrary.com** for more eBooks and Audio. You'll be glad you did.

Suggested Reading

Robert Collier - "The Secret of the Ages"

Robert Collier - "The Secret of Gold"

Napoleon Hill - "Think and Grow Rich"

Annie Rix Militz - Prosperity Through the Knowledge and Power of Mind

Joseph Murphy - Your Infinite Power to Be Rich

Anthony Norvell - Money Magnetism - How to Grow Rich Beyond Your Wildest Dreams

Franklyn Hobbs - The Secret of Wealth

Benjamin Franklin - The Way to Wealth

Julia Seton Sears M.D. - The Key to Health, Wealth and Love

Charles Fillmore - Prosperity

John Seaman Garns - Prosperity Plus

Franklin Fillmore Farrington - Realizing Prosperity

Florence Barnard - The Prosperity Book

James Allen - Eight Pillars of Prosperity

Bernard C. Ruggles - Creative Abundance; The Psychology of Ability and Plenty

Neville Goddard's Interpretation of Scripture

Notes:

Neville Goddard's Interpretation of Scripture

Notes: